From Chained To Changed

From Chained
To Changed

BREAK MENTAL STRONGHOLDS AND
TRANSFORM YOUR LIFE THROUGH FAITH

Tracy Ann Spiaggia

To contact the publisher, visit www.creatspace.com
To contact the author, visit www.slingshothc.com
ISBN-13: 9781542627641
ISBN-10: 1542627648
Library of Congress Control Number: 2017902043
CreateSpace Independent Publishing Platform
North Charleston, South Carolina

Printed in the United States of America

Table of Contents

Dedication

First and foremost, I wish to thank God for His amazing, unfailing love that captures each willing heart so we can finally hear the words we all desperately long for, "I love you just as you are." I cannot imagine this life without Him.

I consider myself one of the fortunate few who can say they have been privileged to experience true, unconditional love—a love that allows me to be my authentic self and still be gazed upon with adoring eyes. It's really what we all want out of this life, isn't it—to be known and, once known, loved still? I am an overly blessed woman. Thank you, Ron, for loving me this way and for always believing in me. You are my home.

As for my treasures, Nicholas, Jack, and Ava. I am not certain you will ever truly know the depths of my love for you because I do not yet know if you will be blessed with children of your own. But, if you are, you will someday understand my heart and you too will love from a part of yourself you do not yet even know exists. I pray God's hand will forever rest on each of you and bless you beyond measure. Love God and one another well all of your lives. That is all I'll ever ask of you.

Acknowledgements

Most importantly, I would like to thank my wonderful family for enduring my long hours these past couple of years and supporting me as I grow. For each of you, I would gladly give my life.

I would like to thank my son, Nicholas, for his contribution to the creation of this book's cover and other graphics. You are indeed a very talented designer with limitless potential. Invite God in and watch Him expand your gifts beyond your wildest dreams! To have crafted this together is fabulously special to me.

I would like to thank South Ridge Community Church, most especially Pastor Nathan Tuckey, for leading me into the most transformational relationship with God one could ever hope for. I have also been so enriched by past and modern greats like Oswald Chambers, A.W. Tozer, C.S. Lewis, Gary Smalley, Timothy Keller, Ravi Zacharias, Andy Stanley, Jimmy Evans, Caroline Leaf, Gary Thomas, Joyce Meyer, John Trent, and countless others. I believe

God still appoints prophets, leaders, and teachers to guide and, through partnership, encourage us on our journeys to God's heart. I am eternally grateful for the wisdom, clarity, and insight I could not have procured on my own.

I would also like to thank Joshua Rosenthal, founder of the Institute for Integrative Nutrition (IIN), for his vigor and resolve in pursuing his vision of a school that would equip those passionate about wellness to change the world, one struggling person at a time. This is God's ripple effect.

Lastly, I would like to thank Drew and Nicole van Esselstyn and Jerry Palmieri for their editorial expertise and honest evaluation of this book. What a gift to have friends and colleagues genuinely vested in my success.

> A wise man should consider that health
> is the greatest of human blessing.
> —HIPPOCRATES

Introduction

> Progress is impossible without change,
> and those who cannot change their
> minds cannot change anything.
> —GEORGE BERNARD SHAW

This is a book intended to provide hope and encouragement, sentiments that flow directly from my heart to yours. It is a culmination of my life's journey thus far and all it has taught me until this day. I naturally am uncertain of the audience God has chosen for it, but most definitely I would have written it had it been just for me, for the arduous process of hand-selecting every word was cathartic and healing. While some of the material may be a bit heavy, the aim is to awaken you to realities that, while easier if ignored in the moment, can inhibit us from ever stepping out into the rich life God intended. I pray, as you choose to turn the pages, you do so with a fully open mind and heart so that you can receive all that God has for you.

Unfortunately, we find ourselves in the throes of one of the worst health crises this nation has ever experienced. "The lives of far too many people in the world are being blighted and cut short by chronic diseases such as heart disease, stroke, cancer, chronic respiratory diseases, and diabetes," according to Lee Jong-wook, director-general of the World Health Organization.[1] The Center for Disease Control and Prevention (CDC) offers these shocking statistics about the epidemic:

"The facts are arresting:

- 7 out of 10 deaths among Americans each year are from chronic diseases.
- In 2005, 133 million Americans—almost 1 out of every 2 adults—had at least one chronic illness.
- About one-fourth of people with chronic conditions have one or more daily activity limitations.
- Mental illnesses and chronic diseases are closely related. Chronic diseases can exacerbate symptoms of depression, and depressive disorders can themselves lead to chronic diseases."[2]

The Center for Science in the Public Interest concludes, "Unhealthy eating and physical inactivity are leading causes of death in the U.S....The typical American diet is too high in calories, saturated fat, sodium, and added sugars, and does not have enough fruits, vegetables, whole grains, calcium, and fiber. Such a diet contributes to some of the leading causes of death and increases the risk of numerous diseases."[3]

Regardless of faith subscription and just from a human perspective, this undeniable calamity should deeply disturb you. We as a people are drowning, in more ways than one. Lifestyle-related diseases are just one manifestation of our vain attempts to self-soothe deep-seated pain. The real issue at hand is man's desperate attempt to feel worthy, whole, and loved in a culture that simply will not and cannot satisfy such needs. Sadly, many look to sources such as food, work, technology, and the like, to fill these nagging voids but to no avail. While this summation will terrify some, I see it differently. I see it as presenting an awesome opportunity to reveal the power and love of God to a hurting and lost population through those He has burdened with the passion to heal. We desperately need a force greater than and outside of ourselves to fill our God-shaped holes once and for all, and He stands at the ready to deliver.

> *Indeed, God is ready to help you right now.*
> 2 CORINTHIANS 6:2 (NLT)

It is up to each of us, however, to yield our hearts, minds, and bodies to His redemptive strength so that we may be made well, understanding it is ubiquitous and unresolved strongholds that truly deny us health and keep us from living our best lives. In partnership, we can go from living a "chained" life to a "changed" life. I'm eager to share with you my view of just how to do that.

Health is a state of complete harmony of
the body, mind and spirit. When one is
free from physical disabilities and mental
distractions, the gates of the soul open.
—B.K.S. IYENGAR

CHAPTER 1

What's Your Style? What's Your Source?

CHAPTER 1

What's Your Style? What's Your Source?

Without a doubt, each of us experience struggles in our lives. Granted, some are more harrowing than others, but we all have burdens. For some of us, it's a chaotic home, faltering finances, a stagnant marriage, or just the daily grind. For others, it's disease, joblessness, a prodigal child, or even death of a loved one. Sure, we can prioritize these on some sort of pain-level scale, but that wouldn't be fair because suffering is suffering and, in and of itself, worthy of compassion.

So, knowing you labor to some degree, the questions become, "How do you manage stress?" "How do you respond to challenge?" "Are you able to achieve balance in your life or are there pervasive troubles that you just can't get in front of?" "Do you shrink back in fear, deny by becoming the ostrich shoving its head in the sand, rage, become emotionally crippled, or rise up against the opposition with confidence and boldness?"

We all have tendencies and comfort zones, many of which lean heavily toward dysfunctional. That's just a manifestation of the world's fallen nature. I would venture to say that none of us can remedy every mishap without error or flaw and that very few of us can maintain simultaneous balance in every area of life. Given the near constant bombardment of triggers and woes, it's just not possible. The goal, then, for all of us ought to be striving each day to react and execute better than the day before. Despite the harsh realities of life, we are all capable of daily improvement, even if it's only by one-degree turns. But, what if you lack the internal wherewithal? From where can you glean strength and encouragement? Once you find that headspring, how can you sustain the daily flow necessary for real impact and growth? That's the impetus of this book, to share with you my source for perseverance, balance, and hope. Together we will explore ways that we can be held back from living our best lives, how to identify specifically those hindrances, how the secular mindset manages strongholds versus how God would have us manage them, and finally, the key components necessary for ultimate, not fleeting or superficial, victory in uncovering the pathway to our highest selves. Let us together go from "chained" to "changed."

Then my enemies will turn
back when I call for help.
By this I will know that God is for me.
PSALM 56:9 (NIV)

Soul! Would you from the battle shrink,
And flee before the foe?
Do you beneath the burden sink,
And in the dust lie low?
Oh! Waste not there vain tears and sighs:
The trumpet sounds are clear;
O'ercome, and to My glory rise!
O'ercome, and triumph here!
—THOMAS H. GILL

The question is not, will there be
difficulties and threats to our existence,
but how will we deal with them and
what can we learn from them. How
can they become blessings to society,
as a life threatening disease is to an
individual, by teaching us about the
meaning of our life and existence?
—DR. BERNIE SIEGEL

Chapter One Notes

CHAPTER 2

Nature vs. Nurture

CHAPTER 2

Nature vs. Nurture

S ome believe that a newborn baby is like a tabula rasa, a blank slate, having no predetermined or inherited traits and that the person he or she becomes is the sole result of collective experiences and surroundings—of nurture. As we delve into the science in this area, though, you will come to understand that's simply not accurate. Beginning in our youth and throughout our lifetimes, we all develop and, over time, engrain certain behavioral and thinking patterns depending on a number of factors. These include, but are not limited to, the frequency and severity of traumatic experiences, the impact on and conditioning of our sympathetic nervous system response and unique perception, the presence or absence of modeled and taught coping skills (be they healthful or impaired), our child-hood experiences (most influential being the home envi-ronment), and our genetics. Both nature and nurture factor into our development and our "slate" does, in fact, have some markings on it straight away thanks to genetics.

Based on these ingredients, our reactions to stressful situations differ. Some retreat into themselves or vices and addictions while others, like me, respond by morphing into something more monstrous than that which threatens them. There are a lot of factors at play when reflecting on the cause and effect of our behavior patterns. First, we must consider our constitutions, which are our inherited natures. Constitution is defined as the physical makeup of the individual especially with respect to the health, strength, and appearance of the body.[4]

While it has always been held that genetics are immutable, and certainly regarding most physical attributes they are, recent developments in the field of epigenetics are refuting that theory with regards to predisposed behaviors, thinking patterns, and disease.[5] It has recently been discovered that it is, in fact, possible to affect changes in our genetic expression but it requires a very high level of self-awareness and an unrelenting intentionality to change. We'll explore this later in the book.

The next factor to consider is your condition, which is the culmination of experiences from the environment in which you were raised and are living—nurture. It is important to note, however, that your condition is also influenced by your constitution or predisposition passed down from mom and dad. For example, if you were raised by two combative, pessimistic parents, it is very likely that you, too, will go through your life with similar behaviors and beliefs, not only because you were raised in that culture but also because the constitution and condition of your parents has exploited your genetic makeup.

Science has recently caught up to scripture in this area. Experts like Dr. Caroline Leaf[6] have concluded that the moment-by-moment choices we make, which ultimately comprise our lives, do, in fact, alter the structure of the brain via a process known as neuroplasticity. Consequently, with altered genetics, we unwittingly pass down these behavioral patterns and life views to our children. These newly discovered truths debunk the tabula rasa premise and corroborate multiple Bible verses, including those citing the iniquities of the father *who opposes God* will be passed down to the third and fourth generations.[7]

Note that, when reading scripture, it is critical to hang on every word. Not a single utterance is trivial. Every word is divinely placed and intended to teach us something. *"All Scripture is inspired by God and is useful to teach us what is true and to make us realize what is wrong in our lives. It corrects us when we are wrong and teaches us to do what is right"* (2 Timothy 3:16 [NLT]). The iniquities of the father are passed down to whom? To those who oppose God. So, we can deduce that by grace and grace alone our iniquities will not be inherited by our children if we align with God, live according to His precepts, and humbly submit to His sovereignty and ultimate authority. I believe this to be true even if you have attained understanding of these truths after you've had children. God's grace knows no bounds. While there is brilliant research in this area, to expound any further would deviate from the purposes of this book. Suffice it to say, though, that independent examination for your own personal growth and understanding is a wholly worthy and fascinating pursuit.

In the forming of the condition, beliefs are adopted—
beliefs that can build up or tear down. They can set us free
or bind us in chains. People in our lives speak messages over
us such as "You are going to do great things one day," "You
have so much potential," or "I love you exactly the way you
are." These kinds of messages cause a life to flourish and
encourage its full potential. These blessings are life giving.
On the other hand, some hear messages such as "Can't you
do anything right?" "You're always in the way!" or "You are
a burden." These curses snuff dreams and choke out that
budding life. Every blight adds a link to the chain that fet-
ters itself ever so tightly to the belief system.

Mind you, these messages don't necessarily have to
be verbally communicated. They can be articulated in a
myriad of ways. Take physical touch as an example. If you
are given lots of appropriate hugs and kisses as a child,
especially from your parents, the message you receive is
"You are loved and worthy." If, on the other hand, you are
excessively hit or even intentionally ignored, the message
is "You are unloved and unworthy." In fact, I opine that
actions have greater influence than words. So, here we
have examples of how a condition is formed, be it positive
or negative.

Now let's look at the far-reaching impact messaging
can have throughout a person's lifetime. If edified and
given unconditional love, a child will grow into a stable,
emotionally grounded adult capable of giving and receiving love, which is the primary calling of every human life.
Wounded and traumatized children will enter adult life
with chains that weight them down and prevent them

from ever stepping into the lives God has for them. They will also be ill-equipped to give and receive love, leaving them empty and hopeless. If they are left in this condition, the despair speaks into the void, resulting in sadness, vain striving, anger, and even rage. This is because a life without love is antithetical to our design. The internal screw tapes perpetually spew the damaging sentiments, affording the lies a louder voice and more authority over time. Now chained, without divine intervention, that person will likely live out his or her days trapped in that condition set as a child, robbed of the fullness of life and sending out a damaging ripple effect to anyone and everyone he or she encounters during his or her lifetime.

Naturally, dysfunctional coping mechanisms are acquired in a futile attempt to protect from further hurt. This is where the coping styles come into play. With this perspective, circle back around to the questions posed at the start. How do you respond to challenge? In trying times, do you shrink, deny, rage, or rise? Your style points to your condition. If you are a riser, good for you—you are one of the fortunate few! Don't take it for granted. Cultivate it. Model it. Share it. Thank who you need to thank for loving you so well. It's a true gift. If you fall into one of the other three categories, we have a bit of work to do. As a recovering "rager," I submit changing your condition is one of the hardest things you'll ever do, and the work never ends. Debunking the beliefs set in childhood is a formidable yet entirely worthy pilgrimage. Indeed, what are your options? The status quo? Accepting your "lot" as immutable, thereby settling into your dysfunction like an easy chair and wounding all of those around you? After all, hurt people hurt people. That simply will not do. By the mere fact that you are reading this book, I trust you agree and are eager for change.

Ideally, we should all strive to better ourselves every day, knowing that our time here is a gift. One of the byproducts of such daily effort is the ability to change the very structure of your physical brain, carving new, healthier pathways from which your thoughts and resultant actions can flow, *remembering that every action began as a thought*. Changing your thoughts leads to change in your condition which leads to change in your constitution, your life, and the legacy for your children and beyond! We all have the potential for such radical change, but we need one key ingredient—love. We were created to love others and ourselves. We need it like we need air to breathe. It is the primary catalyst to positive change. The only way to give love is to get your head and heart right so they can receive it, allowing you to be filled. We cannot pour from an empty cup. I pray you choose to fight for wholeness rather than gimp through life. *"I have set before you life and death, blessings and curses. Now choose life, so that you and your children may live"* (Deuteronomy 30:19 [NIV]). Give yourself permission to dream big of a life free from the chains that bind. Altering your condition and, in time, your constitution requires a minute-by-minute commitment to living another way, in a style that does not come naturally to you. You must become the salmon that swims upstream. That takes fortitude, strength, courage, and, most of all, faith. But know that you were made in the spirit of these qualities. *"For God has not given us a spirit of fear and timidity, but of power, love, and self-discipline"* (2 Timothy 1:7[NLT]). You do not have to manufacture them on your own—they are already hardwired into your being. Together we can rediscover these traits that this life has buried deep beneath layers of fear, hurt, anger, and sadness. In this fighter's stance is where I've been living for the past decade or so. I can testify that lasting change really is a decision to go to war with yourself, but the victory, which is yielded a bit each day, is sweet.

When I examine both my constitution and my condition up until my early thirties, it is plain that I did not always have a flexible, easy-going way about myself, despite wishing I did. More often than not, I was a controlling perfectionist with little grace for others and a mouth primed to put you in your place. In fact, throughout my childhood and even into early adulthood, all I wanted was to become an attorney so that I could argue for a living. I was effective at it, and worse still, it felt good. Unbeknownst to me at the time, I was, in my hurt and immaturity, misappropriating one of my gifts from God. What He intended to be used for His glory, I was instead using to propagate my own prideful agenda, albeit an agenda justifiably borne from pain. While part of me wishes there were some cosmic eraser that could efface those heated exchanges, another part of me wouldn't dare because they're the choices that made me and have incited deep, God-honoring change.

> Every trial that we pass through is capable
> of being the seed of noble character.

> Every temptation that we meet in the
> path of life is another chance of filling
> our souls with the power of heaven.
> —FREDERICK TEMPLE

Each choice we make contributes to the grander story of redemption and renewal God desires to perform in each of us. Without them we would have no testimony to share and inspire. God wastes nothing. As I aged, I became increasingly worn out by arguing—it didn't feel as invigorating as it once did. It was a lifestyle that was exhausting to maintain because we are not designed to live in such a way. We are image-bearers, and when living in opposition to that fixed nature, we tire like an overworked hamster on a wheel. In that weary state, I was able to hear God's voice, wooing me to Himself, pleading with me to lay down my sword and enter into a healing relationship with Him. For the first time, I felt hopeful. In time and through the power of God's Spirit, I was able to self-confront and assess the relational damage. As you can imagine, it wasn't pretty. I know my story is not unique—the details are, but the moral is not. It's as old as time. We are all driven by our ego and its ugly cousins, fear and shame. It's the consequence of the Fall but that doesn't absolve us from personal responsibility. God has, in His mercy, provided all we need to course-correct. He also provided us with the gift of free will. Change is a choice *and* a verb.

Unfortunately, because of our stubbornness, many of us require a catastrophe of some kind to catapult us out of apathy and into positive change—a wake-up call, if you will. For some, it's a health crisis; for others, it is job loss or divorce. In and of themselves, these trials are horrid. When viewed in the larger scale of one's entire life, though, oftentimes exceptional beauty and growth are aftereffects.

This was the case for me. I'm fortunate in that I still enjoy several long-lasting friendships stretching all the way back to grade school. These people mean very much to me. We've matured together, married together, raised our families together, suffered together, and laughed together. Early in our motherhood years, a group of four of us got together at least once a week, enjoying one another's company while our kids tore the house apart. This lasted for several years. In the summer of 2007, one of these lifelong friends, whom I'll call Sarah, suddenly passed away at just thirty-five years old, leaving behind a beautiful family.

I was shattered. Hers was the first death I experienced, outside the natural passing of some elderly relatives. When, as a younger person, you experience an untimely death, it snaps you out of a mindset of immortality and forces you to view your own life as finite and fragile. That's what her death did for me, forever changing who I am and the way I choose to look at life. God is simply amazing that way, how He will use tragedy, something that is not of Him, to affect Christlike change in His children—ashes to beauty. I grieved long and hard, and I am still grieving, truth be told. However, I use my grief. I use it to remind me life is fleeting and that each one of us has a unique and specific purpose, a task assigned before time began. I wanted to start using my time wisely and in a way that pointed others to Jesus Christ because, ultimately, He's all that matters. Her death also awakened me to the reality that many people suffer a lonely existence of feeling lost, desperate, and hurt. I saw, for the first time in my young, self-absorbed life, the massive mission field to simply love and encourage people.

As I continued struggling to make sense out of her death, I prayed to God to reveal answers in His Word that would bring me the assurance I needed to let her go. I randomly opened my Bible to this verse, which I hadn't read before. He is the ultimate Comforter.

> *Good people pass away; the godly often die before their time. But no one seems to care or wonder why. No one seems to understand that God is protecting them from the evil to come.*
> Isaiah 57:1 (NLT)

Through that verse, I knew she was with Him and at peace. As the torment died down and with this newfound contentment, I found my own calling, one that had been camouflaged in a pugnacious disguise. For the very first time, I viewed my personality style not as some loathsome design, which had been seared onto my spirit from the time I was very young, but as a formidable means to share truth as God defines it, not as I do. I became, over time, more focused on taking down the dysfunctional, combative aspects of myself, which required, and still requires, a tremendous dose of self-control. At first, I relied on myself for the discipline and self-awareness. You can imagine how "well" that went. If I had been able to change myself by myself, most certainly I would have done it already. In the short term, I became shamefully aware that, in and of my own ability, I could not change in any significant way. I needed a power outside myself. I chose to surrender to and partner with God and it was, far and away, the best decision I've ever made or ever will make! My prayer is that this book will inspire you to enter into a similar partnership with the only One who can rescue you from yourself. By His love, you can overcome.

> *So letting your sinful nature control your mind leads to death. But letting the Spirit control your mind leads to life and peace.*
> ROMANS 8:6 (NLT)

> *Submit to God, and you will have peace; then things will go well for you.*
> JOB 22:21 (NIV)

> *God will do this, for he is faithful to do what he says, and he has invited you into partnership with his Son, Jesus Christ our Lord.*
> 1 CORINTHIANS 1:9 (NLT)

Chapter Two Notes

CHAPTER 3

Memory of an Elephant

CHAPTER 3

Memory of an Elephant

Indulge me here, if you would, for herein lies some fantastic analogies from which to gain unique insight into the way many of us live. We will examine the practice of taming an elephant and compare the elements and consequences of that process to the effects we suffer as a result of experiencing negativity, hostility, trauma, neglect, and abuse during our lifetimes. This is the scrutiny of the "chained" life.

For as long as I can remember, circuses that include animals have repulsed me. My heart has always bled for the underdog, those without a voice or not strong enough to stand for themselves, be they animals or people. I often wondered why in the world that huge beast didn't trample the trainers in order to break free. Truth be told, any time I skimmed over an image or commercial of these poor creatures dressed in all types of bedazzled costumes, I'd root for the elephant to do just that—crush the trainers. After all, they average ten to thirteen feet in height and weigh between 11,000 and 15,400 pounds![8] With just one swipe of that massive trunk, the trainer would be launched fifty yards to his death, which seems fair to me—the victim overtaking the perpetrator.

Elephants, however, are known as gentle giants and are not, by nature, aggressive animals. Despite harsh treatment, it has in the past been uncommon for attacks like the ones I conjured up in my imagination to occur. But recently, elephants have developed a vengeful side as a result of human brutality.

"*New Scientist* has reported that elephants appear to be attacking settlements as vengeance for years of abuse by humans...Scientists suspect that poaching in the 1970s and 1980s marked many of the animals with the equivalent of post-traumatic stress disorder, perhaps caused by being orphaned or witnessing the death of family members."[9] So, what my research revealed is that elephants have recently been manifesting violent and vengeful behavior against humans for the savagery perpetuated against their herds or family members. "In India and Africa, elephant bulls have been known to attack entire villages, killing people and destroying rural homes. Presently, elephants kill up to 200 people a year in India and up to 50 in Sri Lanka. Elephants have a remarkable memory and many of these killings are inflicted upon villages that were involved in mass culling, even decades prior to the attacks."[10] I interpret this to mean that external factors like cruelty by humans have altered their genetic makeup, and resulted in new, albeit problematic, rage-type behaviors that hinge upon and exploit their God-given gift of a remarkable memory—how striking. "A study by Dr. Poole showed that a lack of older bulls to lead by example had created gangs of aggressive young males with a penchant for violence towards each other and other species."[11]

I'm certain you can begin to connect the dots I am plotting. There are uncanny similarities between the behaviors of elephant and human—wouldn't you agree?—most especially when you consider that the unfavorable reactions in both species originate from having been abused. It has also been established that the brains of humans and elephants are, indeed, similar. "The elephant brain is remarkably similar to the human brain, with as many neurons and synapses, as well as a highly developed hippocampus and cerebral cortex."[12] "Extensive observations have confirmed that elephants indeed remember injuries and hold grudges against their abusers. For example, one study of African elephants found that the animals react negatively to the sight and scent of clothing worn by members of a nearby Maasai tribe of people."[13] Can you relate? Do old, impassioned feelings of revenge rise to the surface at the slightest whiff of the one who hurt you or someone you love? Know that those dark emotions are a chain that keeps you bound to your past.

There's another curious quality about elephants. Perhaps you've heard the expression "She's got a memory like an elephant." Have you ever wondered how this saying developed and if, in fact, it were true that elephants really do have long-lasting memories? It is obvious from the preceding examples that they do, but how else does that trait affect them and the way they live? Admittedly, as I continued my research, I became more and more disgusted with the potential of human beings for barbarity. Despite elephants being the largest land animal in the world, it is quite possible for a human, nearly one-tenth its size, to train, or bring into submission, this massive creature. While it is possible to subdue an older, wild elephant, it's ideal, according to these trainers, to begin the process on the animal's *second* day of life![14] While repulsive, from a pragmatic perspective, it makes sense. Why wait until it has begun to form its independence? Why attempt to undo what it has known to be true up to that point and replace it with opposing commands and expectations, especially those that are punitive and restrictive? Seems less than ideal considering the inherent danger of an average-size man wrangling a three- to seven-ton animal into submission.

The training process includes shackling the elephant with chains first to a wooden structure or in between two trees so it cannot move. Naturally, it begins to flail around attempting to break loose but to no avail. Next, the mahout, a person who works with, rides, and tends to an elephant,[15] beats the animal while talking to it in a soothing voice. Quickly, the elephant's spirit is broken, and it submits. Fear, pain, thirst, and hunger finally make the elephant give up all resistance.[16] In the next phase, the mahout secures the newly broken elephant to what's referred to as a "working" elephant, one that is already broken. It is permitted to bathe in rivers, eat, and drink but only tied to another elephant. After a few weeks, the elephant is permitted to move about in shackles, and is no longer tied to another elephant. In that brief time span, the animal's spirit has been broken and it is now fully submissive to the will of man. This training process is known as elephant crushing.[17]

I realize this is not easy to read, but there is much to be learned from the resemblances just described. Take a moment and ask yourself these questions: "Am I like the elephant, harboring bitterness and rage against those who have hurt me?" "Have I, too, been crushed at a very tender age and chained by a mahout of my own?" "Was there someone in my life who, while beating me with action and word, spoke over me in low, insidious tones ideas of impotence and promises of vanquishment?" For most of us, the answers are unfortunately yes. Sometimes the mahout is intentional in his or her efforts, while others unknowingly set and lock shackles around their loved-ones' ankles. These people are like the working elephants, allowing new recruits to be chained to them, leading them into their own lifestyles of full acquiescence, devoid of independent thinking and aspirations of freedom. It's a travesty either way, a reality you must thoroughly explore and extract if you are to ever live free.

Another key question to ask yourself is "Am I also like the elephant in that my belief system, which confines and restricts, has never been challenged?" On day two of life, when the crushing begins, the elephant in short order surrenders to the belief that it will never ever be free again. Are you like the elephant in this regard as well, having a low threshold for pain and trial, permanently conceding at the first experience of struggle? If it would only tug at the chain, it would know that it held the power to break free all along! But it doesn't. It remains submissive its entire life all because of what it believed the first week of its life. Have you ever tugged at your chains to see if, in fact, they are strong enough to continue holding you back? Perhaps the chains are a fantasy of your own imagination. Possibly, with just a brief yet brave consideration, you will finally be free to change.

What's interesting is the elephant was created with tremendous size and strength. It doesn't have to "do" anything to acquire its power other than just be an elephant. The same is true for us. We have been created with sufficient fortitude to overcome our challenges and also do not have to "do" anything to acquire it. It is simply in us as a testament to God's love and provision. What both elephant and man must do, however, is utilize their innate strengths, tap into them, to be free. Otherwise, the gift of potency is useless. If, though, you continue in a defeatist mindset, chains or no chains, you are bound. With the right partnership centered on focused, intentional, and sustained effort, freedom with finality is absolutely possible! I know because I've experienced it.

There is another way, though, that some choose to live even with the knowledge that they aren't well. For some, a deficit of any kind becomes familiar and even comfortable. It can become your very identity, so pursuing freedom from it would be likened to losing yourself. For some, that idea is not palatable because their dysfunction has become as comfortable as a favorite sweater. A couple of examples might look like a financially destitute person not proactively seeking gainful employment because he or she has come to prefer outside assistance and perhaps even adopted an entitled mindset—chained. Another may have suffered a long-term yet treatable illness and received a lot of help and attention. Rather than aggressively pursue health, he or she settles for a lifestyle of reliance and dependence—also chained. You get the idea. So, the questions now become "Do you want to be made well?" "Do you even want to challenge the chains?"

Curiously, even the elephants can fall into this pitfall. "What most people don't realize is that elephants are very strong and can break out of their chains if they wanted to. However, if the elephant is being cared for, i.e., fed, watered, bathed, and exercised, it has no problem spending some of its time chained."[18] Don't be like the elephant, settling for bare essentials and expecting nothing more out of life. There is very little more gratifying than self-sufficiency.

There's a similar biblical account that will shed God's perspective on the subject. In John, chapter five, we read of Jesus's return to Jerusalem to observe a Jewish holy day. There was a place called the Pool of Bethesda where many sick people congregated in the hopes of receiving healing from Spirit-filled waters. Jesus happened upon a sick man who had been lying there for thirty-eight years! He asked the man, *"Would you like to get well?"* (John 5:6 [NLT]). That seems a peculiar question posed to a man who has spent the majority of his life ill. It is crucial to understand, though, that God never asks a question to get an answer, but rather to get you to think. Of course this man wanted to be made well, but he had grown so accustomed to his impaired condition that he surrendered to it, perhaps even adapted to the point of favoring it. Jesus's question inferred, "Are you willing to partner with Me to receive healing? Are you willing to forgo this life's definition and enter into something new and different which will require effort on your part?" We know this because in order for the man to be healed, Jesus required something of him. *"Stand up, pick up your sleeping mat, and walk!"* (v. 8). Jesus didn't reach down, set His hands under his arms and lift him up. The paralytic had to stand up and collect his things on his own. Jesus spoke into the circumstances, but the paralyzed man had to do his part by acting in faith upon Jesus's promise.

The same holds true for us. We ought not to consider God as a super-natural Santa Claus, believing He will deliver us from all evil without any expectation of partnership on our part. While He most certainly is able to do so, He loves us too much for that. Think of it this way. If you did for and gave to your children everything they ever requested while requiring no contribution on their part, would they not grow increasingly entitled and crippled, in a sense? They would never enjoy the pride that comes with independence and the fruit borne of hard work. We must break the chain of defining toil as something to be avoided; as being inherently bad. Many people equate difficult or strenuous with miserable and simple or effortless with favorable. This is a pitfall with the potential for becoming a stronghold. As parents, we are to prepare our children for hardship and equip them for autonomy and competency if they are to live truly free. God parents us in the same way. He will be the essential wind beneath our wings, but it is up to us to flap our wings and fly. He requires partnership in life just like He does in our faith. He has provided all we need to enjoy eternal life with Him through Jesus's sacrifice, but we can only be certain of our salvation if we confess with our mouth and believe in our hearts that God raised Jesus from the dead.[19]

> Why doesn't God do everything we ask?
> He has done it. The point is— will I
> step into that covenant relationship? All
> the great blessings of God are finished
> and complete, but they are not mine
> until I enter into a relationship with
> Him on the basis of His covenant.
> —OSWALD CHAMBERS

So, if you have been like the elephant never challenging the chains, know that the Devil is in that. Examine the motives behind your indifference. Surely fear is a component, but we know we were not created in a spirit of fear or timidity but in a spirit of courage, love, and self-discipline (2 Timothy 1:7). Know, too, that the more you ignore the inner promptings to change your destructive ways, the less likely it becomes over time that you will ever break free. This is because what you tell yourself becomes your reality. If, upon hearing that gentle nudge, you say to yourself, "Not today; maybe tomorrow," you are solidifying your aversion to effort in that area. Tomorrow leads to tomorrow leads to tomorrow.

"The more often he feels without acting, the less he will be able ever to act, and, in the long run, the less he will be able to feel."[20] You deserve more than an apathetic existence. You were created for abundance. Pray against the fear, break the chain, and wander the lush pastures of life the way God intended. By your choosing, receive and enjoy a new identity of deliverance, capability, and joy.

> If you realized how powerful your
> thoughts are, you would never
> think a negative thought.
> —DR. CAROLINE LEAF

> Be miserable. Or motivate
> yourself. Whatever has to be
> done, it's always your choice.
> —WAYNE DYER

> Your body loves you, but if you do not
> love your life, it will end it far sooner,
> thinking it is doing you a favor.
> —DR. BERNIE SIEGEL

Chapter Three Notes

CHAPTER 4

Idols and False Gods
Secular Experience of Managing Strongholds

CHAPTER 4

Idols and False Gods
Secular Experience of Managing Strongholds

Throughout our lifetimes, we accumulate both positive and negative experiences and, as discussed in chapter one, consequently develop good and bad behavioral patterns. The positive experiences edify and free us, moving us ever forward in the direction of our true selves. As a side note, your perception of having enjoyed such boons has much to do with your mindset and outlook on life. Is your cup half-empty or half-full? There is always much to be grateful for no matter the details. Stop and consider the miraculous physiology necessary for you to be reading and comprehending these words right now. "Thank you, God, for the gift of sight and sound mind." It is a choice to set your mind on the lovely and beautiful, be it much or little.

> *Finally, brothers and sisters, whatever is*
> *true, whatever is noble, whatever is right,*
> *whatever is pure, whatever is lovely, whatever*

*is admirable—if anything is excellent or
praiseworthy—think about such things.*
PHILIPPIANS 4:8 (NIV)

The negative experiences, though, do the exact opposite.
They corrode our mind and spirit, cause us to foster dysfunctional coping mechanisms to soothe the pain, and lure
us to alternate pathways of artificial happiness. The trouble with those paths, however, is that they are always dead
ends—every single time. Some routes prove short with a
steep drop-off at their ends, while other routes are long and
winding. But they both lead to nowhere. Like a rat trapped in
a sealed labyrinth, we just can't find our way out. We scram-
ble, backtrack, and recalculate, growing frustrated and hopeless. Worse yet, as time passes in this condition, we become
increasingly self-focused and isolated which is fertile ground
for the liar to have his way with us. He whispers falsehoods
such as, "If there really were a God, why wouldn't he help
you out of this mess?" "If God were truly good, why wouldn't
He have rescued you by now?" "This is the way your life will
always be." "You are so incompetent; look at your disastrous
life." "Is life even worth living?" On and on he goes, breaking
you down just like the mahout does to the elephant.

Are you familiar with such mutterings? I am. The chains
are strong, the whipping is painful, yet he only speaks in a
whisper. If you let him, he will crush you too. Do not let the
chains become your master. Do not be dragged off into slav-
ery by fear. These are painful things to read and feel—I know.
We've all been there, but, if we yearn for a better tomorrow,
we must step outside our comfort zones and work hard today.

Unfortunately, to quiet the voices, many seek out false gods such as alcohol, drugs, sex, over-work, professional striving, material possessions, food, excessive television, technology, and the like. Truth is, we are all addicts of one kind or another because, at the very least, we are all addicted to comfort. Each of us favors the path of least resistance, the avenue of greatest ease even if ultimately it is not in our best interest. We take the escalator or elevator instead of the stairs. We eat fast food rather than cook a healthy meal from home. We get our "news" from Tweets and posts rather than researching the topic for truth. We sleep in rather than go for a run. We relate to one another through texts rather than through in-person conversation. Just consider the multitude of modern conveniences we employ every day to reduce the amount of effort we must put into anything. Make things as quick, easy, and painless as possible—that's our modern-day motto, and, like any other addiction, it has harmful effects.

There is a myriad of idols we can choose to worship in exchange for empty promises of fulfillment, and we all do to some extent. Without the true living God in our lives, it is nearly impossible to even recognize these destructive imposters working against you because they are disguised as something that tantalizes us, like the glimmering, yet forbidden, apple hanging off the tree in the Garden of Eden, which we'll discuss later in the book. We've all got this caricature in our imaginations of what the Devil looks like, complete with red cape, horns and pitchfork. That's the stuff of fairy tales so don't be deceived. He was once beautiful[21] and comes dressed as everything we've ever yearned for, seducing us into believing his half-truths, his false promises of satiety.

These idols are also difficult to discern because the world's definition of "success" is antithetical to God's definition. The world screams, "Try harder, work faster, fit more into your day, forsake idle pursuits like quiet, quality time spent with loved ones for a few more hours at the office, and strive for a bigger house, faster car, smaller jeans, more "friends," a perfect home, and a flawless existence." Can't you just hear the pressure-filled directives? It seems there is nowhere to be still and just breathe! No way to escape the chaos. This is how the enemy works, though. He's in the shadows, accusing and devaluing, taking you apart brick by brick. He typically doesn't come at us guns blazing because he's easier to spot and combat that way. He knows it's more effective to be illusive and somewhat inconspicuous because if his affronts are undetected day by day, in the end, he will have you. A slow fade is most often better than an aggressive assail at destroying your life, which is his ultimate goal (John 10:10). "Indeed the safest road to Hell is the gradual one—the gentle slope, soft underfoot, without sudden turnings, without milestones, without signposts."[22] Allow me to offer you a hypothetical yet relevant example here.

I'm a man in my twenties, feeling immortal as most young people do. It is in that mindset I establish very poor lifestyle habits such as unhealthy diet and inactivity because, after all, a young body is quite resilient. At thirty years old, I marry and she too shares these same habits. For a few years, we enjoy free rein, giving little consideration to the consequences we'll surely suffer later in life. For now, all that matters is today, and today is fun and easy. Fast-forward eight years and we've got two children, ages five and three. They are full of energy and, like all children, want desperately for my wife and me to join them in their ruckus. Sadly, we can barely keep up because we are both extremely over-weight and deconditioned. One poor meal choice at a time, coupled with a lifestyle of inactivity, we have invited illness and disease into our still-young lives, which prevent us from engaging with our children to the degree we would all prefer. Each meal over those many years presented us with a choice, and each time we capitulated to temptation. In the moment, the decisions seemed inconsequential, even trivial. But today, we realize our physical condition is a culmination of all those poor choices. We are all suffering the consequences of many years of bad choices, but two suffer though they are innocent. It is very painful having to tell our children, "We cannot play kickball with you because we're too tired and can't run" or, "We can't go to the zoo today because Daddy's knees hurt and Mommy needs to lie down." Because we did not prioritize fundamental lifestyle choices like diet and exercise, we have all been robbed of what matters most in life—relationship, joy, and love. If we choose to continue in these habits, the thievery of these blessings will compound, our children will likely be orphaned at premature ages, and perhaps our grandchildren will never know their grandparents.

Does this fictional yet highly plausible depiction help you see how our day-to-day choices matter and how they will impact your future freedoms? Does it also lend some insight into the insidiousness of poor daily decisions and how one more trip through the drive-through or refusal to just go for a walk matters? Calamity of this nature doesn't happen overnight; it's typically experienced as a result of a gradual letting go of priorities—of procrastination and neglect. Does this incite righteous anger when you consider all that has been taken from you and those you love? You cannot change your current circumstance unless you feel burdened by holy discontent, even to the point of disgust and indignation. Use those vexations not to plunge deeper into bondage, but to set your sights on your chains and resolve to do whatever is necessary to cast them off and be free. Stewardship of all areas of your life is deeply spiritual, when pursued with God-honoring intentions. Do not compartmentalize these things as if diet and exercise are over here and God is over there. He is omnipresent and should be considered in everything we do. Honor Him in every aspect of life so that when He calls you to service, you are prepared and equipped to go. Each decision is either taking down one of your life's bricks or cementing one in place. It's up to you to build your fortress so that it's strong and impenetrable rather than look down one day in your vulnerability at the rubble piled at your feet.

> The awareness that health is dependent
> upon habits that we control makes us
> the first generation in history that, to a
> large extent, determines its own destiny.
> —JIMMY CARTER

Rather than feel condemned or angry about perceived similarities in the details of your own life, which is most definitely not of God, recognize who your real enemies are: Satan, the world, and your old nature. All of these forces desire to lure you away from stewardship and into eventual destruction.

> *For our struggle is not against flesh and blood, but against the rulers, against the authorities, against the powers of this dark world and against the spiritual forces of evil in the heavenly realms.*
> EPHESIANS 6:12 (NIV)

I pray these words will awaken you to the reality that a battle rages on for your very soul, a battle you cannot see with your eyes but can feel internally as you wrestle every day to move towards what you instinctually know to be good and right. That is the pull of the Father, drawing you ever closer to Himself. Know that God has gone before you and has put to death our enemy (John 19:30). All you need to do is *choose* to partner in the victory.

What are the whispers of God, though? God's Word says:

Enter My rest.	Psalm 23
Be still and know I am God.	Psalm 46:10
Look to Me for your worth and value.	Psalm 139:13-17
Stop striving in your own effort.	Galatians 3:3
Stop worrying and know I am your Provider.	Matthew 6:25-34
You are beautiful just the way you are.	Ephesians 2:10

I know the great plans I have for you.	Jeremiah 29:11, Psalm 138:8
Seek peace that surpasses your understanding.	Philippians 4:7
You are enough.	2 Corinthians 3:5
I do not condemn you.	Romans 8:1
I forgive you.	Isaiah 43:25
I love you.	Isaiah 43:4, John 3:16

Now those are words to live by! Just reading them, don't you feel released, even if only for a moment? Permission is granted to get off the hamster wheel and just be. That's love in its purest form—being truly accepted exactly the way you are, here and now. No criteria or conditions to meet—just be yourself. The world demands change from the outside in—through our own effort, which is utterly exhausting and most often futile. With God, however, change comes from the inside out because it is the indwelling transformative power of God that, over time and through divine partnership, breaks the power of strongholds, sets us free, and ultimately reveals our truer selves. Remember, though, that discerning God's voice is only possible when you steward your body well, so in a state of quality health, you can hear. You must make intentional efforts to quiet the noise in your life that drown out His neutral, sometimes even low, tones.

Many Christians have so busied
themselves with programs and

> activities that they no longer know
> how to be silent and meditate on
> God's word or recognize the mysteries
> that are in the Person of Christ.
> —RAVI ZACHARIAS

God is always the perfect gentleman, never forcing Himself onto us or shouting to demand our attention.

> How does God transform a life, a
> family, a nation, the world? Quietly.
> Without fanfare or fireworks. Where
> He is allowed in, He enters. There
> the changes happen. Addictions are
> broken. Marriages are restored. Broken
> hearts are mended. Ruined lives are
> restored. New hope is uncovered.
> —*ALONE IN GOD'S PRESENCE*, 2011[23]

He instead waits ever so patiently for us to harken His call. *"Look! I stand at the door and knock. If you hear my voice and open the door, I will come in, and we will share a meal together as friends"* (Revelation 3:20 [NLT]). We must create the quiet, calm environment in our personal worlds that best facilitates reception.

> *I listen carefully to what God the*
> *LORD is saying, for he speaks*
> *peace to his faithful people.*
> PSALM 85:8 (NLT)

When we fail to hear His voice, it is not
because He is not speaking so much
as that we are not listening…We must
learn to be very attentive, in order to
hear God speaking in His ordinary
tone without any special accent.
—CHARLES H. BRENT

To discern God's voice, you should engage in daily meditation and prayer, methodically quieting the body and mind. Establish the intimate routine of reading your Bible every day, even if just for a few minutes. "A Bible that's falling apart usually belongs to someone who isn't" (Charles Haddon Spurgeon). Consider such practices as Sabbath, God-designed regular patterns of rest, for the brain. For most, this requires a tremendous amount of intentionality and discipline. This is just one of the many benefits of partnering with a faith-based health coach so that new, life-giving disciplines can be learned and integrated into your life.

Regarding the damaging sentiments roused by the accuser's messages, we can be certain that God offers us truths to contradict his lies. Since there are countless examples throughout scripture of people feeling contemptible before God, let's go all the way back to the beginning, to the Garden with Adam and Eve. This is where it all began. In the book of Genesis, we read of the perfection that was the Garden of Eden. Adam and Eve lived *with* God, His being walking among them—visible and tangible! They were created into an environment of pure joy and peace, into shalom, something we as mortals will never know until we reach heaven. In Genesis 2:25, we read, *"Now, although Adam and his wife were both naked, neither of them felt any shame."* This is because they had not yet been tempted, and the Garden was perfect. In the very next verse, however, we read, *"The serpent was the shrewdest of all the wild animals the LORD God had made"* (Genesis 3:1 [NLT]). The following few verses illustrate the way Satan tempted Adam and Eve into doing the one and only thing God had forbade them to do, which was eat of the tree of knowledge of good and evil. They had free reign but for this one caveat. Consider how skillful Satan must be if he was able to convince God's first two created human beings living in utter bliss that God was not trustworthy and loving. There was absolutely no evidence to corroborate this accusation, but still they both bought it. The moment they forsook God by eating the fruit of the tree, they felt the emotion that drives all other ill-conceived emotions: shame (Genesis 3:7). For the first time, they recognized they were naked and hurried to cover themselves in fig leaves. Before this, they knew nothing of nakedness, shame, or hiding their true selves behind something for the sake of disgrace or embarrassment. These emotions are the direct result of Adam and Eve having expressed their free will by refusing God's authority, renouncing His one and only precept, and forging their own way. Make no mistake, though. We are no different from Adam and Eve. We are *all* guilty of turning from the perfect ways of God and instead traveling down courses of our own choosing, often time with grievous results. *"I did find this: God created people to be virtuous, but they have each turned to follow their own downward path"* (Ecclesiastes 7:29 [NLT]).

In the next verse, God asks them a question. I reiterate that God, being omniscient, never asks a question to get an answer but rather to evoke our contemplation. *"Who told you that you were naked?"* (Genesis 3:11 [NLT]). See what God is doing here? He knows full well that by falling prey to Satan's temptation, they would instantly become aware of good and evil. But I believe He needs them to conclude on their own that it was Satan who informed them of their nakedness and deceived them into a fallen condition. First, this will make them acutely aware of this foe who will war against them and all humanity from that point on and, second, it will help them conclude their autonomous actions have consequences. What does this mean, and why is it problematic? In God's view, for us to have full knowledge of good and evil is to have full knowledge of *all* things. The problem with that is that while human beings have fantastic capacity to choose via free will, we lack the moral wherewithal to always choose what is right and good. Enter sin. God wanted so much to spare us from the fallout of sin, but, despite living in paradise with only one condition, Adam and Eve concluded that that condition was too restrictive.

Does this help you see how having full understanding of everything sends us spinning? Although we are created in God's image, we are far from God Himself. We simply cannot properly manage this enormous and seductive responsibility. Omniscience is an honor reserved exclusively for God. On the one hand, we feel so entitled to know and have it all, but on the other hand, it is a load far too heavy to bear. This is an important lesson to recall when, for His good purposes, He chooses not to reveal all of the whys to us. We can't handle His full disclosure because His ways are higher than our ways and His thoughts higher than our thoughts (Isaiah 55:9). Operating with degrees of blind faith facilitates trust, a key ingredient in *authentic* relationship. Oftentimes, though, living the way Adam and Eve did with a healthy measure of autonomy, we err and resultantly compensate for our unavoidable mismanagement. The deep-rooted knowledge that we fall short, everyday in nearly every way drives that rectification, and it is therefore often-times ineffective. Our depressive state drives us to self-soothe in ways that often worsen our condition. This is how we embark down paths of idol worship. Remember God's first commandment? *"You shall have no other gods before me"* (Exodus 20:3 [NIV]). He issues this directive not because He's a narcissist, but because He knows such a misprioritization will set us on a sure course for death. Just go back to the few most common examples of idolatry and deduce for yourself that to place your trust, worth, and affections in anything other than God will lead to your demise. Let's briefly expound on the likely fallout of each one.

Alcohol and Drugs: Numb and dull the senses, lead to regrettable behavior, destroy relationships, may result in job loss, wreak havoc on the body, steal potential and deny a future, result in a life of isolation and despair, enslave children and future generations in addition, cause disease, and may even cause death.

Sex: Intimate relations outside marriage, in dysfunctional excess, driven by dominance or insecurity lead to lifelong regret, unplanned pregnancy and all that goes with it, disease, loneliness, shame, social stigma, depression; relations can be mismanaged inside marriage as well leading to discord, erosion of trust, and even divorce; adultery can lead to disease, broken homes/relationships.

Overwork/Workaholism: Lost time with family and loved ones, destroyed relationships, exhaustion, depression, perfectionism, futile comparison, neglect of responsibilities outside work, and hopelessness.

Material Possessions/Excessive Spending: Financial ruin, depression, destroyed relationships, greed, discontentment, anxiety, over-work, cluttered home environment, and envy.

Food: Weight issues, lifestyle-related illnesses and diseases, eating disorders, depression, anxiety, body-image issues, and neglected and broken relationships.

Excessive Television and Technology: Loneliness, isolation, depression, social anxiety, wasted time, lifestyle-related illnesses and disease, under achievement, missed relational opportunities, and neglect of daily responsibilities.

All of these vices are mere temporary pain soothers, like taking a Tylenol for a slow-growing tumor. Perhaps you can mask the pain for a very brief time, but nothing is being done to destroy the mass. Not a single one of them addresses the real root of our problems, which is feeling inadequate, unworthy, and irredeemable. Every single one of these forms of idolatry results in a host of desperate consequences like depression, anxiety, anger, rage, physical and mental illnesses and disorders, broken relationships and homes, destitution, and so forth. Worst of all, they all lead to separation from God. When you read the first half of John 10:10, you will be able to see Satan's hand in all of this. *"The thief comes only to steal and kill and destroy..."* (NIV). Through subtle, in-the-moment temptations that exploit our addiction to comfort, the enemy is able to convince us that one more drink, hit, sexual encounter, promotion, meal, purse, movie, or game will do the trick. No, it won't! Each time we surrender, we climb one rung lower into the pit. As we descend, he is able to surreptitiously destroy our lives. If instead we listen to the call of the Father, we can begin to climb up one rung at a time out of the pit and into an abundant life. This is Jesus's promise in the second half of John 10:10. *"I have come that they may have life, and have it to the full"* (NIV).

However, you must partner with God, identify and get focused on your idol(s) of choice, and resolve to become militant about taking them down. Not by your own strength, though. If you could have made yourself well and whole on your own, you would have done it by now. I certainly couldn't do it on my own, not even for a day! Still can't. Daily partnership with God was the essential component to real, lasting change. It remains the single most important relationship in my life. For comparison, let's take a look at a biblical account of someone who never wavered in his trust of God's ability to go before him and deliver victory.

When I have really transacted business
with God on the basis of His covenant,
letting everything else go, there is no
sense of personal achievement— no
human ingredient in it at all. Instead, there
is a complete overwhelming sense of being
brought into union with God, and my life
is transformed and radiates peace and joy.
—OSWALD CHAMBERS

Chapter Four Notes

CHAPTER 5

David and Goliath
Biblical View of Managing Strongholds

CHAPTER 5

David and Goliath
Biblical View of Managing Strongholds

I t was 1025BC when David was just a fifteen-year-
old shepherd boy, born the last of eight sons to Jesse.
They lived in Bethlehem and were part of the tribe
of Judah. At this time, a war raged between the Israelites
and the Philistines. Each army remained in its own
camp, separated by the Elah Valley, hurling threats to
one another. The Philistines had a formidable weapon in
Goliath, their champion who came from Gath to defeat
and enslave the Israelites. The Bible describes him as
follows:

> *He was a giant of a man, measuring over
> nine feet tall! He wore a bronze helmet and
> a coat of mail that weighted 125 pounds. He
> also wore bronze leggings, and he slung a
> bronze javelin over his back. The shaft of his
> spear was as heavy and thick as a weaver's
> beam, tipped with an iron spearhead that*

weighted fifteen pounds. An armor bearer
walked ahead of him carrying a huge shield.
1 SAMUEL 17:4-7 (NLT)

By all accounts, this was a terrifying man. Goliath was posted at the edge of the valley to taunt the Israelites into battle with him, and him alone. This is what he shouted. *"Do you need a whole army to settle this? Choose someone to fight for you, and I will represent the Philistines. We will settle this dispute in single combat! If your man is able to kill me, then we will be your slaves. But if I kill him, you will be our slaves! I defy the armies of Israel! Send me a man who will fight with me!"* (1 Samuel 17: 8-11 [NLT]).

Valley of Elah[24]

It is stated that *"for forty days, twice a day, morning and evening, the Philistine giant strutted in front of the Israelite army"* (1 Samuel 17:16 [NLT]). No member of the Israelite army was courageous enough to step forward to fight Goliath. The two armies would rush each other from their respective camps towards the valley, but once the Israelites got closer to Goliath, they retreated. *"As soon as the Israelite army saw him, they began to run away in fright"* (v.24). Now, as I stated earlier, David, being just fifteen years old, was not part of King Saul's army. His three oldest brothers were, though, so, from time to time, David's father, Jesse, would instruct David to bring the brothers and other officers some supplies, such as grain, bread, and cheese. He was asked to do this at the same time this standoff was taking place, obviously unbeknownst to Jesse and David. Once he arrived on the scene, he heard the battle cries and rushed out to the front lines to find his brothers. It was then he first learned of and saw Goliath. As the Israelites retreated from Goliath, the soldiers explained to David, *"Have you seen the giant? He comes out each day to challenge Israel"* (v. 24). They went on to share about the grand reward King Saul offered to anyone who killed Goliath.

David's next question affirmed for me that he indeed had a heart for God, had the Israelites' best interests in mind, and was not motivated by self-gain. He asked, "Who is this pagan Philistine anyway, that he is allowed to defy the armies of the living God?" He didn't say "Oh man, I get to marry one of his daughters *and* have my whole family exempt from taxes? That's awesome—let me at him!" Instead, he was clearly offended at Goliath's gall to dishonor God's holy name. That's what motivated him to be the one and only man to offer himself as opposition to the Israelites' threat.

However, before David could make his offer, his oldest brother, Eliab, became angry that David was even there. *"What are you doing around here anyway? What about those few sheep you're supposed to be taking care of? I know about your pride and dishonesty. You just want to see the battle!"* (v. 28). Talk about sibling rivalry!

David replied, *"What have I done now?"* (v. 29). This implies Eliab frequently belittles and accuses his brother David of ill intentions and actions. David's frustrated tone comes through in the text of his reply; he is tired of being on the defensive with his brother, having always to explain himself. In my view, what also comes through in this text is Eliab's insecurity when it comes to his brave, capable, and much younger brother, David. I believe Eliab becomes immediately threatened at the mere presence of his brother, most likely because David rises to challenge, whereas perhaps Eliab does not, causing him feel less of a man.

If we back up a bit in the book of Samuel, we'll gain some additional insight to his brothers' disdain toward him. In chapter 16, we read of Samuel's efforts to identify God's replacement of Saul for king of Israel. God instructed Samuel to go to see Jesse, David's father, in Bethlehem. When Samuel saw Eliab, he immediately assumed he'd be the next king because of his appearance. God said no. Samuel asked for the next son, Abinadab. God said no. Next was Shammah and God once again said no. Samuel went through all the seven brothers but none of them were God's chosen one. Knowing God had chosen one of Jesse's sons as the next king, he asked Jesse, *"Are these all the sons you have?"*

Jesse's reply was, *"There is still the youngest, but he is out in the fields watching the sheep"* (v.11). Imagine how degrading this must have been for David. His father didn't even deem him worthy of consideration and left him out in the field tending the sheep. That's tough. Consider, too, how all the older brothers must have felt as Samuel rejected each of them.

The spear in the heart comes when Samuel sees David and hears from God, *"This is the one, anoint him"* (v.12). To me, this helps explain the hostility between the brothers. However, God *chose* David. He didn't ask for kingship. He most certainly never tried to usurp his brothers. He had a God-appointed destiny, and he simply received. If Eliab were confident in his own calling and worthiness, the feelings of jealousy and insecurity wouldn't have been roused.

Getting back to the battle, we now have a better understanding of why Eliab used public humiliation and shame to thwart his brother's intentions of battling Goliath. At the center of Eliab's heart are fear, insecurity, and self-preservation; this is the opposite of David's heart. King Saul got word that David was on the front lines asking questions about the giant, so he sent for him. Immediately upon entering King Saul's courts, David proclaimed, *"Don't worry about a thing. I'll go fight this Philistine!"* (v.32).

Rather than offering a response of relief and encouragement, Saul, too, tried to tear David down. *"Don't be ridiculous! There is no way you can go against this Philistine!"* (v.33).

I love the next verse. *"But David persisted"* (v.34, emphasis added). That's it, dear reader! That's the crux of this entire book. Despite every effort to instill fear into David and cause him to retreat just like every other Israelite in Saul's army at that time, David persisted. This begs the question "How?" How is it that David was able to persist with such a daunting mission? Pay attention, now. This is the key to David's success and yours. David *partnered* with God. He partnered with the God who had been faithful throughout his life, albeit brief at this point. Based solely on David's age, he couldn't have had all that much material to base this huge faith on, but it was enough to propel him into battle with the most terrifying man of that day.

Over the next several verses, David made his case to King Saul. He told him of all the times he protected his father's herd from predators. *"When a lion or a bear comes to steal a lamb from the flock, I go after it with a club and take the lamb from its mouth. If the animal turns on me, I catch it by the jaw and club it to death. I have done this to both lions and bears, and I'll do it to this pagan Philistine, too, for he has defied the armies of the living God! The LORD who saved me from the claws of the lion and the bear will save me from the Philistine!"* (vv. 34-37).

You should read your Bible. It's chock full of thrilling stories like this one. Let's drill down a bit on these verses. First, it is safe to deduce that there are always predators lurking in the shadows, not just for sheep and lambs, but for all of us. For David to have been so effective at destroying these animals, he had to be on guard all the time. Had he allowed himself to be distracted or sleep through an attack, one of the flock would have perished. As their shepherd, he simply would not have that, so he kept his guard up and remained alert. We too must remain alert for attacks on our peace as well. *"Stay alert! Watch out for your great enemy, the devil. He prowls around like a roaring lion, looking for someone to devour. Stand firm against him, and be strong in your faith"* (1 Peter 5:8-9 [NLT]).

Next, notice how David says he immediately goes after the animal and, by force, takes back what's his. He didn't become paralyzed with fear, look the other way as if the attack wasn't taking place, or ask someone else to do it. He stood firm in his faith and attacked back with the fullest confidence God would go before him. He was proactive! He went on the offensive at the first sign of a threat. He didn't wait until the lion had torn the limbs off his sheep, but rather he refused any harm come to them at all. When the animal fought back, he amped up his offensive and tore its jaws apart. Gruesome, I know, but effective. He destroyed that which attempted to destroy him and what he loved.

But, the most important take-away is the "why." Why was David the victor every time? He answers that question for us. "The LORD...saved me." He knew full well in and of his own strength, he would have perished long ago going after beasts like that. But David never operated in his own strength. He always drew his courage from the LORD. It's important to note here that the scriptures read LORD, not Lord. We see both used throughout the Bible, but when we see all capitalized letters, it denotes a personal God, Yahweh. David enjoyed a deep, personal relationship with God and relied solely on Him for all things. That's the pinnacle all of us ought to strive for.

After hearing David's plea, Saul relented and permitted him to fight. Saul strapped David up in his own armor, including his bronze helmet, coat of mail, and sword. After taking just one step in Saul's gear, David said, *"I can't go in these. I'm not used to them"* (v.39). Saul clearly did not have the same confidence and resolve as David, or else he'd have let him go fight in his own tradition. He doubted. Instead, Saul's fear and skepticism show as he tries to send David out in his own style of doing battle. This is an important piece on which to expand. As we face trials in our own lives, people around us will tell us if, when, and how to fight. Their intentions are likely good, but the truth is, each of us must make the final decision for ourselves. We all have our personalized styles and what works for one may not work for another. There is definitely a bio-individual component here, meaning what's best is as unique as our fingerprints.

It's prudent to seek counsel from trusted sources and apply what fits, but you have to make the ultimate decision how to best war against what opposes you, keeping paramount Ephesians 6:13 (NKJV) *"Therefore take up the whole armor of God, that you may be able to withstand in the evil day, and having done all, to stand."* The only non-negotiable component of your armor of choice is the power, truth, and partnership of God. As per usual, David did not yield, trusting that, just as God had delivered him in the past, He'd be faithful to do it again. Defeat has little to do with the "armor" you choose, but rather much to do with the level of trust you place in God to do your fighting for you. Most certainly you need to be a proactive participant in the effort, and throughout scripture, God insists on that, but it is God who ultimately delivers you from foes. Consequently, David did what he knew, what had worked in the past, and that was to collect five smooth stones for his sling. Off he went into war.

Before we delve into the details of the ensuing battle, consider something. As you grapple with these insights, note what David did *not* do: rely on or continue in a pattern that did not work for him in the past. Many of us become ensnared here. We continue doing the same thing expecting a different outcome, which is the very definition of insanity. That familiar giant repeatedly rises up in our lives, and rather than taking the time to examine what was and was not effective in overcoming in the past, we drudge on in old, ineffective patterns hoping for different results. If we are ever to be free, that mind-set must be changed. Consider the pathway of water. It will always take the avenue of least resistance. That's all fine and good for water, but we as Imago Dei beings, created in the image of God, must acknowledge that we have been set apart for great works and are capable of more than we can ever dream or imagine. We can excavate new routes for our thoughts and ultimately our actions and need not travel down the same old trails that always lead to disappointment and failure. We need to engage in an internal dialogue with God, expressing our thanksgiving and confirming His truths. By that exercise we pick up our shovels and carve out new paths to victory while the weeds grow over and eventually erode the old, fruitless paths.

Here are a few verses for you to meditate on. Commit them to memory so that when temptations arise, you are armed with God's truth. Remember, every time Jesus was tempted by the Devil, He defeated him with scripture.[25] When combatted with God's Word, the Devil must flee.[26]

So humble yourselves before God. Resist
the devil, and he will flee from you.
JAMES 4:7 (NLT)

For as he thinks in his heart, so is he.
PROVERBS 23:7 (NKJV)

For I know the plans I have for you,"
declares the LORD, "plans to prosper

you and not to harm you, plans to
give you hope and a future.
JEREMIAH 29:11 (NIV)

If any of you lacks wisdom, you should ask
God, who gives generously to all without
finding fault, and it will be given to you.
JAMES 1:5 (NIV)

Trust in the LORD with all your heart
and lean not on your own understanding;
in all your ways submit to him, and
he will make your paths straight.
PROVERBS 3:5-6 (NIV)

Be very careful, then, how you live—
not as unwise but as wise.
EPHESIANS 5:15 (NIV)

You need to persevere so that when
you have done the will of God, you
will receive what he has promised.
HEBREWS 10:36 (NIV)

I can do all this through him
who gives me strength.
PHILIPPIANS 4:13 (NIV)

He gives strength to the weary and
increases the power of the weak.
ISAIAH 40:29 (NIV)

*Finally, be strong in the Lord
and in his mighty power.*
EPHESIANS 6:10 (NIV)

*But those who hope in the LORD will renew
their strength. They will soar on wings
like eagles; they will run and not grow
weary, they will walk and not be faint.*
ISAIAH 40:31 (NIV)

*My grace is sufficient for you, for my
power is made perfect in weakness.*
2 CORINTHIANS 12:9 (NIV)

*The LORD is my strength and my
defense; he has become my salvation.*
PSALM 118:14 (NIV)

Once David collected his stones from a stream and gathered his sling and staff, *"He started across to fight Goliath"* (v.40). See how proactive he was? Goliath was the one doing all the taunting but, David made the first move toward the battlefield. That's how a hector generally works. They goad and torment, but, like a small dog who's all bark and little bite, rarely deliver the ultimate consequence they threaten.

As with all scripture, take care to read the next verse slowly so as not to miss any important nuances. It reads, *"Goliath walked out toward David with his shield bearer ahead of him, sneering in contempt at this ruddy-faced boy"* (v.42). Pick up on anything? Goliath had his shield bearer go out ahead of him when he could plainly see David did not have a shield bearer. See how the antagonist isn't as strong as he portrays? He needed protection and the boldness of another to go before him in order to step toward the very war he himself began. There's only one reason for that—fear. He knew that any man willing to offer himself as a ransom for his people was far more courageous than he would ever be. I believe Goliath began to doubt himself—he began to break. We all know that when someone hurls insults at others, this behavior is a direct reflection of that person's own insecurities. Like the bully on the playground, those who seek out opportunities to tear others down are actually the ones suffering the most. It seems Goliath was no different. "Ruddy-faced boy." What does that mean? Well, ruddy means having a face red in coloring, flushed, rosy. With the term "boy" following that adjective, Goliath was emphasizing David's youth and inexperience, demonstrating insult at even the suggestion of being pit against such a novice—again, insecurity.

Goliath cursed David by the names of his gods which naturally yielded no impact because they are false. He then commanded David to *"come over here and I'll give your flesh to the birds and wild animals!"* (v.44). Again, Goliath would not offensively move toward David. He instead instructed David to move toward him, even with a shield bearer between them, again revealing his fear.

David's reply oozes confidence and resolve. *"You come to me with sword, spear, and javelin, but I come to you in the name of the LORD Almighty—the God of the armies of Israel, whom you have defied. Today the LORD will conquer you and I will kill you and cut off your head. And then I will give the dead bodies of your men to the birds and wild animals, and the whole world will know that there is a God in Israel! And every-one will know that the LORD does not need weapons to rescue his people. It is his battle, not ours. The LORD will give you to us!"* (vv.45–47). Don't you wish you were there to witness this historical fight? Like being ringside for Rocky's first win! You root for the underdogs, most especially when you know they deserve victory because their hearts are right. I so appreciate how David retorts back to Goliath the very same threats he made, thereby using Goliath's tactics against him as if he dug his own grave. It's as if David is saying, "Oh yeah, you're going to give *my* flesh to the birds and wild animals? Like hell you are! In fact, I'm going to give *your* flesh to them, along with your head."

Notice David never once implies he alone will defeat Goliath, but is very careful to give full acknowledgment and glory to God. *"I come to you in the name of the LORD Almighty,"* *"Today the LORD will conquer you,"* *"The LORD does not need weapons,"* *"The LORD will give you to us."* When we defer all opportunity for victory to the only One who can deliver, He is faithful to do so.

"As Goliath moved closer to attack, David quickly *ran out to meet him"* (v.48, emphasis added). Goliath moved closer, yes, but David *ran* toward his enemy, seemingly devoid of doubt or trepidation.

> If there by lying before you any bit
> of work from which you shrink, go
> straight up to it, and do it at once. The
> only way to get rid of it is to do it!
> —ALEXANDER MCLAREN

He knew from the moment he first heard of this Goliath that God would empower him to destroy him. David never lost that resolve, that myopic focus to crush that which tried to oppose his king. *"Reaching into his shepherd's bag and taking out a stone, he hurled it from his sling and hit the Philistine in the forehead. The stone sank in, and Goliath stumbled and fell face downward to the ground"* (v.49). Remember David collected five smooth stones? I guess he wanted to be prepared, but did he really think it would take God until the fourth or fifth stone to hit Goliath in just the right spot? Of course not. First stone, first shot...down! Face down! The next verse (v.50) reads, *"So David triumphed over the Philistine giant with only a stone and sling"* because *"the LORD does not need weapons."* The next verse reflects the vengefulness of the elephant that we all can manifest at times. David's retribution is righteous, though, because Goliath came against God. *"And since he had no sword, he ran over and pulled Goliath's sword from its sheath. David used it to kill the giant and cut off his head"* (vv. 50–51). What irony. Do you think Goliath considered for even a moment that morning as he dressed for battle that the very sword he loaded into its sheath would be used to sever his own head just hours later?

Let's tease all this out. What did David have that is also available to us? First, steadfast faith that was not compromised by fickle feelings or circumstances. David was not a fair-weather friend of the Lord. Remember, he was the last of eight sons and was therefore relegated to herding the sheep while his oldest brothers enjoyed the glory of defending their beloved country, Israel. That had to play with his ego a bit. I'm confident his brothers were quick to repeatedly remind him of his place in the ranks, too, no different than any other family. Additionally, as a shepherd boy, David had nothing but time on his hands to stew about their rivalry and give the Devil a foothold. Instead, I conclude he used all of his time praising and worshiping God. His faith is the proof.

What are your circumstances? Do you give the Devil an inroad by lamenting over the less-than-ideal details of your life rather than living in a spirit of holy gratitude for all that's good and right with your life? The most efficient conduit to evil is ingratitude for it births a multitude of sin. On the contrary, the most efficient conduit of God's grace and love is pure thanksgiving, for it is impossible to be a defeatist while giving God His due praise. *"Give thanks in all circumstances; for this is God's will for you in Christ Jesus"* (1 Thessalonians 5:18 [NIV]). David was so young at this point, but he must have stewarded his days with excellence based on all the godly fruit he exemplified by the age of fifteen. No matter where you are in your own life, you can start right now living as David lived so that you too can hold high the severed head of what comes against you. Sickness? Call it by name and have God use you as His instrument to cut off its head! Divorce? Bankruptcy? Crippling insecurity and fear? Whatever is robbing you of your best life, call it by name and ask God to slay it. Partner with Him. He loved David no more than He loves you. So, He'll move for you in the same way He did for David. If it's hard for you to trust that, then you need to spend more intimate time with the Lord. That's the only way to uncover for yourself His true, immutable character and unconditional love for you personally. As you read and reread biblical accounts of His faithfulness, it will eventually seep into your soul that He is the great I AM and that He cherishes *you* and wants the fullest life for *you*. All He asks for is a repentant and yielded heart—an invitation to His love and power in and over your whole life. Together, chains are broken.

There is another helpful angle from which to consider this scriptural account of David and Goliath. David could have reacted differently to Goliath's threats. What if David responded like everyone else by shrinking and refusing to fight? What would have been the Israelites' fate? Most certainly they would have become slaves of the Philistines, forever changing the course of history. Because of one man's courage to step out in faith, an entire tribe of people were spared enslavement and set on God's intended course. What if we took that macroexample and honed it into a very realistic microexample? What if a father was facing a giant that threatened the safety and well-being of his family, like an addiction, an affair, a lifestyle-related disease, or financial peril? He too would be faced with two choices: run from the threat, leaving behind his family to be leveled by his cowardice or truly own the responsibility as leader of the home and take that giant head-on.

The first choice would lead to the destruction of not just his life but also the lives of his loved ones and, worse yet, likely kick off or perpetuate a genealogy of bitterness, struggle, and disadvantage. The second choice, however, if he partnered with God, would result in eventual rescue, an intact family that would likely be stronger than before, a genealogy of resilience and faith, self-confidence, and a bolstered spiritual life. We are all faced with such choices every single day. We can either be the elephant stuck in the beliefs and fears of its past, never challenging the chain and surrendering to its perceived restrictions or we can elevate up and over the limitations of an animal and realize that we are designed to question limiting beliefs until we experience the epiphany that we have all been gifted the key to unlock every chain! The beautiful thing about scripture is its quality of transference into our own lives. The reason God inspired the words He did was so that we could better understand His nature and vast love. The Bible is a love letter to all of us. What He did for one of His own back then, He'll do for any of His children today. That same power is available to us in the here-and-now. All we have to do is receive.

> *Don't be afraid of the enemy! Remember the Lord, who is great and glorious, and fight for your brothers, your sons, your daughters, your wives, and your homes!*
> NEHEMIAH 4:14 (NLT)

> Being reminded about the incredible power of God's love, and living as He intended, is the most powerful motivation to change.
> —RICK WARREN

Chapter Five Notes

CHAPTER 6

The Key to Today's Trust Is Recalling
God's Faithfulness of Yesterday

CHAPTER 6

The Key to Today's Trust Is Recalling God's Faithfulness of Yesterday

As you embark on the essential journey of intentional gratitude, consider what the Jews did during Old Testament times to recall and reflect on how God had already moved in their lives. Let's take a brief look at the account of Joshua leading the Israelites across the Jordan River (Joshua 1–4). God appointed Joshua to lead His people across the Jordan River so that the Israelites could take the land God had promised them. Joshua instructed everyone to follow a half mile behind the Levitical priests, who would be carrying the Ark of the Covenant of the Lord, and to purify their hearts beforehand in preparation of God doing great wonders and miracles (Joshua 3:1–6).

Before going further, it's important to point out that, without them purifying their hearts through confession and a renewed consecration to God, He would not be able to move on their behalf. Perhaps that's confusing. Consider it this way. You are a parent with two children. You happen upon them fighting. Once they are separated, you learn the older sibling has attacked the younger for taking his toy. Instantly, there is a gap between you and the oldest because of the harm he has caused your youngest and the way he chose to resolve the issue. If in that very moment, your oldest asks for something, you likely wouldn't consider helping him because of the estrangement caused by the offense. If, however, he instead came to you and your younger child with genuine regret and a wholehearted apology, you would be able to reconcile and likely extend the grace to give him what he asked for. That's a very simplified explanation of the purpose of confession, to get yourself right with God again when you've offended another

There's a big difference between us as prideful humans and God, though. We tend to seek the apology so we feel vindicated. I believe He seeks the confession for two selfless reasons. First, to provide an opportunity for us to reflect on our sin so that we, in our remorse, may choose to rid ourselves of it. God's ultimate desire is to fashion and shape us with the help of His law and through the grace found in Christ into the person He originally intended so that we are free to live without regret or shame, having loved ourselves and others well. Second, to once again display His limitless capacity for forgiveness and love, a trait He so desperately desires us to manifest to one another. How beautiful that He never grows weary of our ebbs and instead rejoices in our flows, our reconciliation, every single time. No different than when your own child misbehaves. He or she offends you. You both are now alienated. Then your child, in and of his or her own free will, seeks you out to apologize and ask for forgiveness. No matter the offense, your heart swells and you are brought immediately back into right relationship with your baby. It's the same concept with God. He yearns to be and stay in right relationship with us, enough to die.

Back to the story. The Israelites did as instructed, and the next day they followed the priests to the river. As soon as the priests' feet touched the water, the river receded despite being at its highest level of the year. The priests carried the Ark to the center of the river's bed and stopped. The waters were held back, the ground was dry, and God's people crossed safely toward the land of Jericho! Here we witness another divine partnership. Without the Ark, the priests' feet would have been no different than the Israelites' feet—wet—but, by carrying the Ark of the Covenant of the Lord, God was with them, and He and He alone parted the waters. We can rejoice being on this side of the finished work of the cross because *we* are the temple of the living God. He resides in us now, not in the Ark. When our feet touch the water's edge, He reveals dry ground for us to safely traverse.

Once on the other side of the river, rejoicing in God's victory for them, Joshua instructed the twelve men he appointed to represent the twelve tribes of Israel to go to the center of the Jordan River and bring out twelve large stones that they would set and display to serve as a memorial of the great works God had done there. *"In the future, your children will ask, 'What do these stones mean to you?' Then you can tell them, 'They remind us that the Jordan River stopped flowing when the Ark of the LORD's covenant went across'"*

(Joshua 4:6–7 [NLT]). The standing stones would remind the Israelites for generations to come of the goodness and faithfulness of God.

Now, go back to 1 Samuel 17:34–37. As David is making his case to King Saul pleading to take on Goliath, what does he do? He recounts all the times God delivered him and his sheep from the jaws of the predatory animals. Think of it—a fifteen-year-old boy chasing down a hungry lion that has his sheep in its mouth, clubbing it, and tearing its jaw apart. I have a son the same age….It ain't happening! The only way David could have been so bold was to have partnered with God in a myriad of smaller ways throughout his life, eventually building up his courage to such an unthinkable degree that grappling with a bear was now within his wheelhouse. That build-up happens one way: as new threats present themselves, you recall how God delivered you before and you go. You don't waiver. Don't give doubt room to play. Hesitation reveals weak faith.

Today we need to do the same thing. We need to erect our own standing stones so that, in times of trouble, we can calm our spirits by remembering all the times God was faithful to deliver us in the past and then act. This reflective exercise is critical in building a strong faith, the kind that is not easily dismantled in times of distress.

Being a writer of sorts, I love to journal. My journals are one example of my personal standing stones. When I'm facing a giant, I again partner with God and read through past accounts of His faithfulness. This refreshes my gratitude and trust. Then, I stand tall, pressing into His past and future promises, relying solely on His omnipotence to set my stone square in the center of my enemy's head. And He has done just that every single time. Other examples of standing stones for me include pictures that remind me of a difficult season out of which I have risen stronger, plaques with empowering and encouraging statements, framed scripture verses, sticky notes with quotes and verses that are applicable to my current circumstance, pieces of jewelry, certain songs, books and other writings, and the like, all that remind me of the finished work of Jesus.

I am intentional, too, to carve out quiet time with each of my children to remind them of God's goodness in their own lives. We'll reflect on a challenging time in their life and give thanks, over and over again, to God for delivering them. We recall the sicknesses He healed them from, the sticky situation with friends that He prompted them to mend, the looming exam, the fear of joining a new team or starting in a new school, and so forth. This is so important, because it cultivates their belief in and trust for God for themselves, preparing them to soon step into their own relationship with Him independent of Mom and Dad.

Take some time to dream up your own standing stones, reminders to bring you back to the center of God's heart day by day. Interact with these everyday, pray over them, not as idols, but as physical symbols to center and ground you in His truths as the world's lies try to overwhelm you.

I have another personal example that's worth sharing. Growing up, we were very tight with a family in town. In fact, my parents had been friends with their parents since early grade school. They are family. One night about four years ago, the phone rang around 3:00am, which is never good.

"Your uncle has had a severe heart attack. The doctors say he won't likely survive."

Now, remember back in the very beginning of the book where I discussed how we all respond to challenges? It used to be that I mimicked my familial influences. I would panic, overreact, and dive headlong into the worst-case scenario. That was my go-to. But thankfully God is still in the business of re-creating. I have been in serious minute-by-minute partnership with Him for fifteen years at least. He has done a redemptive work in me, painstakingly carving off those bits that don't belong. This reaction style was one of those bits. When my family conceded my uncle likely wouldn't survive, I refused to accept that. We went to the hospital and witnessed a desperate family terrified at the idea of losing their patriarch. We all wept. I asked if I could pray over him. My cousin and I went to his bedside. I prayed over him the only way I knew how, and that's intense, convicted, and with God's authority. I articulated my refusal to accept the doctors' prognosis and my belief that it was God's will to heal my uncle. Nurses watched with confused and doubt-filled faces. We wept again.

Can you guess what happened? In response to all our ardent prayers, God stared into the situation and healed him. My uncle is still with us today and has resumed most of his normal life. I would imagine there isn't a day that goes by when every member of that family doesn't pause to thank God for the gift of their dad and husband. Once he was home, I bought my cousin a gift; a beautiful painting that read, "*Give thanks to the LORD for He is good! His mercy endures forever*" (Psalm 118:1). I suggested she hang it in a prominent place in her home and use it as a standing stone of God's faithfulness to heal and restore her family. She sent me a picture shortly thereafter showing me where it is hung in her family room. That's a standing stone! This is what I'm encouraging you to do in your own life. Set them all around so that when the waves crash against the hull of your life's boat, you will not capsize.

Another exercise to cultivate your trust in and relationship with God is to create a vision board at the start of each year or newly committed season of life; this is another wonderful benefit of partnering with a faith-based health coach. This is an exercise I encourage my clients to do with me, and it has always resulted in daily renewed motivation to keep plodding along towards their unique goals. A vision board will provide inspiration for your future, whereas the standing stones help you reflect on God's faithfulness in the past. To do this, you can gather magazine clippings, photos, quotes, favorite scriptures, personal writings, images, and so forth that depict the goals you have identified for yourself in the coming year. Arrange and affix these items to a board of your choosing and hang it somewhere prominent where you will see it throughout each day. Whenever possible, stand before it and pray. Give your hopes and dreams to God, for He is able and willing to bless you with them. Recite the verses you selected and commit them to memory. Speak out loud the promises of God and how you wish to see them manifest in your life.

For example, if this is the year you want to finally quit smoking, choose a scripture like, *"For God has not given us a spirit of fear and timidity, but of power, love, and self-discipline"* (2 Timothy 1:7 [NLT]). By repeating this out loud and committing it to memory, you activate its inherent power in your life. The self-discipline you've desperately tried to manufacture on your own but failed will now flow from the only Source able to bring deliverance from such a formidable stronghold. Our words have tremendous power! Going all the way back to Genesis again, we read that God *spoke* creation into existence. "*Then God* said, '*Let there be light.' Then God* said, '*Let there be space between the waters.' Then God* said, '*Let the waters beneath the sky be gathered into one place so dry ground may appear'*" (Genesis 1:1–29 [NLT]). There are nine verses in the first chapter of Genesis alone that comprise God's spoken command of creation. Being fashioned after God, we can deduce that our words also wield tremendous power over our lives and the world around us. The Bible has over one hundred verses confirming this.[27] Every time you speak, you are either blessing or cursing. I encourage you to take some introspective time to assess the manner in which you speak to yourself and others throughout your day. If you have pessimistic and negative tendencies, give this area to God. Invite Him in to change the way you speak. This will, in turn, change the way you think, which will, in turn, change the way you live and manifest God's power in your life.

What can be more unkind than to
communicate our low spirits to others, to
go about the world like demons, poisoning
the fountains of joy? Have I more light
because I have managed to involve those
I love in the same gloom as myself?
—FREDERICK W. FABER

Ask yourself "What brings me to complaining the fastest and most often?" Traffic, a cold, piled-up laundry, or a long line at the grocery store? These are all quite trivial but can be exaggerated into something we deem worthy of excessive protest. This disposition becomes a giant that needs to be slain. A complaining spirit erodes our health and the health of those we drag under our cloud. Our complaining can be likened to second-hand smoke, poisoning those around us. *"Do all things without grumbling or questioning"* (Philippians 2:14 [ESV]). *"Let no corrupting talk come out of your mouths, but only such as is good for building up"* (Ephesians 4:29 [ESV]). *"A joyful heart is good medicine, but a crushed spirit dries up the bones"* (Proverbs 17:22 [ESV]). The most efficient behavior to lead you out of this pattern is thanksgiving and praise. Next time you feel the impulse to complain about the rain, for example, stop and remember that rain is life giving. Without it, we'd die. Give Him thanks for it rather than grumble about your soggy shoes. It's all about your perspective.

> Oh, that we could reason less about
> our troubles and sing and praise
> more! There are thousands of things
> that we wear as shackles which we
> might use as instruments with music
> in them if we only knew how.
> —L.B. COWMAN

Perhaps you are now asking what measures you can take to begin effecting such changes. A reasonable question from someone wanting to stop smoking would be, "Well, what practical things can I do after I invite God's power into this resolution to quit?" After all, we need pragmatic application to all the concepts I am proposing throughout this book. There are a couple of viable steps you need to take every time you feel that urge to light up. First, share your commitment with those you love and trust. Remember, partnership is key. They will hold you accountable in love and cheer you on as you work. Next, stop whatever you are doing and pray. Pray with passion and confidence. *"Let us then approach God's throne of grace with confidence, so that we may receive mercy and find grace to help us in our time of need"* (Hebrews 4:16 [NIV]). Next, you must repeatedly execute a healthy habit in place of the unhealthy. So, rather than have a cigarette, go for a walk, eat an apple, listen to uplifting music, journal your struggle, snap a rubber band left on your wrist to break the addiction pattern in the brain, try acupuncture, meditate, ask yourself leading questions like, "Why am I craving this right now? What triggered me? Will this cigarette destroy or enrich my life? Will it add a brick to my life's fortress or tear one down? Do I *really* want to be free? Is surrendering to a momentary urge worth the regression? Is this cigarette my master or am I its master? Are there people in my life who love and rely on me and want so much for me to be healthy?" and so on. It doesn't matter which healthy exchange you choose, just choose wisely and choose it every time.

Lastly, visualize that cigarette as the chain it is. Envision a literal shackle around your ankle, robbing you and your loved ones of the freedom that comes with health. Let that anger wash over you and use it. Anger in and of itself is not sinful, provided it is righteous. It's what we do with it that determines whether or not its sinful. You've been handed the key to unlock that chain, but it is up to you to choose to use it! Little by little, as you apply these techniques, your old ways will die off and you will have adopted a new, healthy habit in its place. All glory goes to the Father who empowered you to reign victorious over this stronghold. The deeper your admiration grows for Him, the more you are sanctified into the likeness of His perfect Son, the more beautiful a person you are to be around, the more whole you become, and the richer your life experience is. It's the most natural and beautiful way to live, on a journey of metamorphosis, redemption, and witness!

We use God's mighty weapons, not
mere worldly weapons, to know
down the Devil's strongholds.
2 CORINTHIANS 10:4 (NLT)

If I believe in God, in a Being who made
me, and fashioned me, and knows my
wants and capacities and necessities
because He gave them to me, and who is
perfectly good and loving, righteous and
perfectly wise and powerful—whatever
my circumstances inward or outward
may be, however thick the darkness
which encompasses me—I yet can trust,
yes, be assured, that all will be well,
that He can draw light out of darkness,
and make crooked things straight.
—THOMAS ERSKINE

Chapter Six Notes

CHAPTER 7

Identify Your Goliaths
What Threatens Your Best Life

CHAPTER 7

Identify Your Goliaths
What Threatens Your Best Life

*Are you worshiping false gods? Soldiers
don't get tied up in the affairs of
civilian life, for then they cannot please
the officer who enlisted them.*
2 TIMOTHY 2:4 (NLT)

What are your "giants"? A habit you
cannot break? A temptation you cannot
resist? If we compare ourselves with our
difficulties, we will always be overwhelmed.
Faith looks away from the greatness
of the undertaking to the greatness of
an ever-present, all-powerful God.
—DAVID ROPER, *OUR DAILY
BREAD*, 8/20/2016

N ow that we have fleshed out the ideas of limiting
beliefs and idolatry as roadblocks to living your
best life, consider the circumstances of your life.

What belief system have you been subscribing to and is it healthy? If not, it's best to rewind all the way back to the beginning, as far back as your memory will go, to identify its origin. That's your starting point for extraction and replacement. Who was your mahout(s)? How did they convince you to adopt their position? Was it aggressive or subtle? What was the messaging? Were you told you weren't good enough, smart enough, thin enough, capable, or worthy? If so, try to remove your emotions from the examination process and look at it more logically. For many of us, revisiting our childhoods can dredge up some uncomfortable and even painful memories. The reality is, though, that this is typically the season of life in which our dysfunction roots are.

You can keep shaving off that stubborn hair at the skin's surface, and for a while your skin will look smooth. But that same hair will eventually grow back. To rid yourself of it permanently, you must extract it from the root. When you do that, there's no need for shaving anymore because the whole hair has been removed. No longer must you focus your energies on examining the spot or making sure it isn't unruly. With it permanently removed, you can shift your focus to other undesirable hairs, eventually ridding your face of them all. The ultimate goal through this reminiscent exercise is to view yourself as a child, but outside yourself—as if the child version of you is with you in the room. Ask him or her how he or she is, what he or she is sad about, afraid of, or angry for. Let him or her tell all. Do not let your ego interrupt. Just listen. Journal these thoughts and ideas that bubble to the surface. Something happens to us physiologically when we free trapped emotions and memories by getting them from head, to heart, to paper. They are released, in a sense. That's why journaling is so powerful—it uncaps the brewing volcano of suppressed memories and sentiments, allowing us to feel unburdened. Many scientists and other medical experts believe that most of the illnesses and diseases we suffer today are a direct result of past wounds left to fester and grow. This is, in my opinion, an intriguing theory worthy of its own book—even shelves of books.

> The truth about our childhood is stored up in our body, and although we can repress it, we can never alter it. Our intellect can be deceived, our feelings manipulated, and conceptions confused, and our body tricked with medication. But someday our body will present its bill, for it is as incorruptible as a child, who, still whole in spirit, will accept no compromises or excuses, and it will not stop tormenting us until we stop evading the truth.
> —ALICE MILLER

Once you've thoroughly assessed the needs of your younger self, be that person to *you*. Be the person you needed most when you were young—encourage yourself, forgive yourself, release yourself from condemnation and guilt, and tell yourself that you are wonderful exactly the way you are. Envision yourself crouched down, nose to nose with that younger self in a genuine attempt to soothe him or her from all these painful feelings. Be kind to yourself, gentle, and loving. Also, forgive those who have hurt you for forgiveness is at the epicenter of God's heart. It is the express lane to true health and peace. That is why there are at least 127 verses on the topic. As per usual, modern science is catching up to biblical truths once again. According to the Mayo Clinic, as well as a whole host of other reputable medical authorities, forgiveness can result in health benefits such as:

- healthier relationships;
- greater spiritual and psychological well-being;
- less anxiety, stress and hostility;
- lower blood pressure;
- fewer symptoms of depression;
- stronger immune system;
- improved heart health; and
- higher self-esteem.[28]

To those of us who truly believe in a Designer who, in His mercy, left us with an instruction manual for life, this is of no surprise.

Next, I would encourage you to consider the naysayer's own past and identify the experiences that may have caused him or her to acquire his or her own negative ways. This typically affords a generous measure of grace and empathy because you realize they too were once wounded and therefore ill-equipped to love others well. Consider the following exercise. Write down all the hurtful messages they spoke over you and place them in a column on the left side of a piece of paper. Draw a line down the center.

On the right side, write the truth that opposes the lie spoken over you. If this does not come easily for you, I would strongly encourage going to God's Word for your truths, for they are the only ones that we can put all our weight on. Here's an example that is similar to what I would do with my clients.

You are unlovable.	**Zephaniah 3:17** *The LORD your God is in your midst, a mighty one who will save; he will rejoice over you with gladness; he will quiet you by his love; he will exult over you with loud singing.* **1 John 4:7-8** *Beloved, let us love one another, for love is from God, and whoever loves has been born of God and knows God. Anyone who does not love does not know God, because God is love.*
You are stupid.	**Genesis 1:27** *So God created mankind in his own image, in the image of God he created them.* **Psalm 147:5** *Great is our Lord and abundant in strength; His understanding is infinite.*
You will never accomplish anything.	**Jeremiah 29:11(NIV)** *'For I know the plans I have for you,' declares the Lord, 'plans to prosper you and not to harm you, plans to give you hope and a future.'*

At first, it may feel uncomfortable, even unnatural, to believe these truths over the lies that have been communicated to you throughout your life, each one of them a link in your chain. Sadly, it is much easier for us to receive and believe the negative opinions about ourselves rather than the positive. Typically, when someone praises us, we squirm, but through daily quiet time with God and intentional work to break down strongholds, you will gradually accept genuine laud not from an egotistical perspective, but from a humble one that affirms God's perfect adoration for each of us.

Consider this view. If you are a parent, you know the intense unconditional love you feel for your child. If your child spoke negatively over him or herself, saying things like "I'm ugly," "I'm a loser," or "I'll never do anything good with my life," your heart would be crushed. This is because you see and believe the exact opposite for him or her. If your child, on the other hand, affirmed in humility his or her true nature as capable, lovely, and beautiful, you would be gratified. Now, transpose this viewpoint onto God and intensify it ten thousandfold. When you speak disparagingly over yourself and allow others to do the same, it robs your joy and grieves God's heart immeasurably.

> *Who are you, a mere human being, to*
> *argue with God? Should the thing that*
> *was created say to the one who created it,*
> *"Why have you made me like this?"*
> ROMANS 9:20 (NLT)

Reconsider your opinion of yourself and know that what you focus on grows. In other words, wherever you choose to place your mental energies will expand. If you focus on the negative, it will thrive and someday likely overcome your spirit, much like ivy consuming a neglected house. Similarly, if you focus on the positive—the truths of God concerning your inherent worth—these will germinate in your spirit and result in burgeoning health over time. You have complete autonomy here. You and you alone possess the ability to determine the direction and momentum of your thought life.

> Thoughts are mental energy; they're the
> currency that you have to attract what
> you desire. Learn to stop spending that
> currency on thoughts you don't want.
> —WAYNE DYER

In order to build something new, like your self-image, you must corral your thoughts much like a herder would his cattle, forcing them in an edifying direction. Once you have procured dominance over your beliefs and ideas, the body will follow suit. In this way, you literally change the structure of your brain.[29] It is then, with sound mind connected to God, that you gather your five smooth stones and aim them one by one at the giants that threaten your peace and joy. God will set them with the force and precision necessary to destroy.

Now that you have done the onerous work of identifying your limiting beliefs and their origins, discern the coping behaviors you have acquired in an attempt to escape the pain. These are your idols. They must be clearly defined in order to dethrone them. When the ghosts return, do you jump in the car to go shopping, to the bar, back to work, through the drive-through, or to a remote location to cut or shoot up? Don't slam the book shut. I realize how painful this process is because I've gone through it myself. Again I pose the question, "What are your options?" Most certainly you can choose to remain in your condition, but don't gloss over or dismiss the inevitable consequences suffered by those around you if you do. Instead, rise and take responsibility for yourself. Don't be like the paralytic lying in wait for thirty-eight years or like the elephant willing to be shackled provided its mahout brings it food and water. No matter how long you have been in your condition or how old you are, it is never too late to be reborn. The reason you continue to draw breath is because God is not finished with you. He has a plan of redemption for us all. Like the shepherd leaving his ninety-nine sheep behind to find his lost one, the woman tearing apart her home for her lost coin, and the father *running* to embrace his prodigal son[30], God is feverishly pursuing you. He longs for you to know your inherent worth and to live a life that rests confidently in it. In faith, pick up your smooth stone, set it in your sling, ask God for the precision and might to launch it with impact, and watch your giants fall.

Even as you scurry to fill your void traveling dead-end roads, God sees your efforts squandered on a lie and has compassion. "*'Can anyone hide in the secret places so that I cannot see him?' declares the LORD. 'Do not I fill heaven and earth?' declares the LORD*" (Jeremiah 23:24 [NIV]). The Trinity witnessed from the heavens our lostness and was so grieved by it that God sent His perfect Son, blameless in every way, to step down, reveal the depths of God's love in a form that would not terrify, and die the most horrid death, so as to make a clear path back to Himself. You are never too far gone. You can never out-behave God's grace. Jesus would have fulfilled His ministry of salvation, even if it were just for you and you alone. That's the incomprehensible vastness of His heart for yours.

As these words penetrate your spirit and inspire change, even just the first steps toward it, know that it is wholly counterproductive to lament over your past mistakes. It's a futile and sapping mental merry-go-round that will surely impede your positive momentum. The truth is that you'll only be again chaining yourself despite having just been freed from bondage. If God casts all your sins as far as the east is from the west[31] and never considers them again, how much more should we do the same?

> Don't be content with spending
> all your time on your faults, but
> try to get a step nearer to God.
> —Francis Raphael

Trust the process and be gentle with yourself, realizing this is a lifelong journey, not an overnight destination. You must learn to live differently. That takes both time and patience. Celebrate every victory, no matter how small. When you falter—not *if* you falter—don't become so downcast that you give up on yourself.

> There is no effort without
> error or shortcoming.
> —Theodore Roosevelt

If you impose a standard of perfection on yourself, you are doomed at the start. Mistakes are valuable ingredients to the evolutionary process.

> The value of action is that we
> make mistakes; mistakes show
> us what we need to learn.
> —PETER McWILLIAMS

Instead, when you err, stand up, dust off, let the past stay where it belongs, and move forward, head held high believing God for renewed strength moment by moment.

> Strive to be as a little child who, while
> her mother holds her hand, goes on
> fearlessly, and is not disturbed because
> she stumbles and trips in her weakness.
> —FRANCES DE SALES

> Who does not know what it is to
> rise up from a fault—perceived,
> confessed, and forgiven—with an
> almost joyous sense of new energy,
> strength, and will to persevere?
> —H.L. SIDNEY LEAR

Chapter Seven Notes

CHAPTER 8

Step out in Faith
Action Steps for Creating Your Best Life

CHAPTER 8

Step out in Faith
Action Steps for Creating Your Best Life

The God of Israel is He that gives
strength and power to His people.
Psalm 68:35 (NKJV)

No, dear brothers and sister, I am still not
all I should be, but I am focusing all my
energies on this one thing: Forgetting the
past and looking forward to what lies ahead.
Philippians 3:13 (NLT)

Soldiers of Christ arise,
And put your armor on,
Strong in the strength which God supplies
Through His eternal Son.
—Charles Wesley

Among the many benefits of spending
time with God, one of the most
exhilarating is the freedom that He
provides in forgetting past mistakes.

Everyone has skeletons in their closet
that they wish they had the power to
evict. Only God can effectively deal with
the memories that haunt us, that hunt
us down in the moments of solitude and
rob us of our peace. How does He do it?
How does God help you forget the past?
He does it by giving you a new identity-a
brand new beginning. You become a new
creation with a redeemed history and a
brilliant new future. Spending time with
God in His Word, you discover that your
way of thinking is being renewed. You
find yourself preoccupied with learning
how to love more adequately, how to be
more generous, how to rejoice even in
the midst of adversity. Spending time
with God in meditation, you find that
your desires change. You long to please
Him, you discover great delight in
obedience, and you experience the joy
of serving others. Memories are healed,
in part because you become so wrapped
up in God you find it hard to recall what
life was like before you knew him.
—*ALONE IN GOD'S PRESENCE*, 2011[32]

S triving to maintain balance in our lives is a God-
honoring pursuit, one that will assuredly yield our
best selves. *"And every man that striveth for the mastery*

is temperate in all things" (1 Corinthians 9:25 [KJV]). When attempting to establish balance, we must first determine all the areas over which we have a high measure of control. The Institute for Integrative Nutrition (IIN) identified twelve areas it deemed essential to health, and those areas are: Spirituality, Career, Home Environment, Physical Activity, Home Cooking, Joy, Creativity, Finances, Health, Relationships, Social Life, and Education. I appreciate and have been inspired by these immensely.

For my style of coaching, however, I included some additional lifestyle areas I feel are just as important in achieving wholeness according to our Creator's design. I call it my Wellness Pyramid.

I arranged these areas in a pyramid to illustrate the slight prioritization necessary to ultimately achieve full wellness. While all sixteen lifestyle areas are essential and significant, it would be nearly impossible to apply the advice offered in this book without prioritizing our thought life first, followed by our diet, sleep and physical activity, as these behaviors and choices set the body in homeostasis, allowing it to optimally perform all its other functions. These four aspects of living are wholly interconnected and codependent.

> To keep the body in good health is a
> duty, otherwise we shall not be able
> to keep our mind strong and clear.
> —BUDDHA

For example, as a health coach, I would be less inclined to first address clutter in the home if my client was busy consuming the Modern American Diet (MAD). I would not be able to successfully challenge his or her beliefs on clutter without first rectifying the physical limitations a diet devoid of nutrition presents. The addiction to sugar, for example, would impede the ability of his or her body and mind to engage for any length of time on lifestyle areas less fundamental than the physiological.

I chose the areas I did for the third level not because they are any more or less important than those in the fourth but because they are an ever-so-slightly higher priority, in my view. Allow me to explain. Like most couples, my husband and I began our lives together with *very* minimal resources. Lots of pasta back then. When I consider all my own life experiences in light of building this pyramid, I opined that it would first be essential to have areas like my finances, my career, relationships and self-care addressed before I would be able to tap into other areas such as creativity, social life and volunteering, for example. Let me state it this way. If I had to work two and even three jobs in order to meet my monthly expenses, which we'll assume for purposes of this example are reasonable, I would not have the free time to volunteer, especially if I wanted to steward a more fundamental need like sleep. It is easy to assign higher priority to some areas while neglecting or devaluing others. The truth is, though, that God created us for balance and stewardship in *all* areas.

You'll notice one of the differences between IIN's model and mine is that, in mine, spirituality is not listed within the pyramid. This is because I perceive God as an essential, all-consuming presence to the entire model and His power is represented by the swirls that encompass the whole pyramid. For health to exist in each area and for them all to symbiotically interact, God must be integrally prioritized. Is He invited into every area of your life? Are there certain areas you have yet to surrender to Him or in which you don't even believe He belongs? Are there areas you have never even considered relevant and have thereby totally neglected? As your Designer, God's intention is to have every facet of life full to overflowing (John 10:10). His design was never for mediocrity or, worse yet, depletion in any area of your life. If you ask, He will reveal which areas need His power to be healed and set right. As you take an introspective survey of your life, you will conclude there are both areas of strength and weakness. To ignore the deficits for the sake of championing the competencies is to eventually succumb in all areas because we can only carry the burden of the deficiencies so long. In and of our own strength, we have limitations. With God, though, we do not for He carries the load and gives us what we need to fortify those fragile spaces that threaten our abundant life.

When you partner with God and a faith-based health coach, the model is used to establish a starting point by determining the top two or three areas of greatest need. Interestingly, though, when there are multiple glaring areas of lack, they tend to adversely affect all the rest. Even when one or two areas of our lives are going well, the other problematic areas drag them down. It's akin to the saying "You are only as strong as your weakest link." Those weakest links become your goliaths. Strategies to eradicate them are crafted in the partnership of client, God, and coach, but it is ultimately up to you, the client, to execute, just like it was ultimately up to the paralytic to rise and take up his mat. To reiterate, there are a few key areas that require daily attention and stewardship in order to achieve fullness over the entire model, though, which are (1) diet, (2) sleep, (3) physical activity. The most critical, however, is our thought life, for it affects every single aspect of our existence, including our relationship with God.

> *For as he thinks in his heart, so is he.*
> PROVERBS 23:7 (NKJV)

If the message of this book influences you the way I pray it does, what will be required most of you is full acknowledgment of how your current way of thinking antagonizes your spirit. In other words, if your thoughts are antithetical to God's truths, you are unknowingly contributing to your maladies simply by agreeing with and yielding your physiology to them. "It is doubtful whether any sin is ever committed until it first incubates in the thoughts long enough to stir the feelings and predispose the will toward it favorably" (A.W.Tozer).

Are you thinking things like "I'll always be poor just like my parents," "Everyone in my family is overweight, so of course, so am I," "I just know I'm going to die young," "Most couples in my family divorced, so my marriage won't likely last either," or "I'm never going to amount to anything so I need to stop pining for my dream career and just stay stuck in the job I have now." Oh, how dangerous such notions are! You mustn't believe everything you think. Heed the wisdom of Marcus Aurelius: "Our life is what our thoughts make it." Even an angry disposition, which is in and of itself antagonistic and sinful, has it's roots in offenses obsessed over again and again, which trains the mind to constantly think upon such things.

"The quick-tempered man is one who habitually broods over wrongs and insults and thus conditions himself for the sudden fit of temper that seems to have no mental origin" (A.W.Tozer). This was my poison of choice and admittedly still offers some appeal given the right circumstances. But, when I fail, and most certainly I still do, I repent, ask for forgiveness from the one I offended, and immediately force my mind back under submission to God. This results in less and less regrettable episodes. All the aforementioned statements and temperaments are bred from a defeatist mindset and will surely entrap you via a self-fulfilling prophecy process. These are the kinds of thoughts you must master. You've heard it said that you can't stop birds from flying over your head, but you can keep them from building a nest in your hair.

> *More than anything you guard, protect*
> *your mind, for life flows from it.*
> PROVERBS 4:23 (CEB)

> *We demolish arguments and every*
> *pretension that sets itself up against the*
> *knowledge of God, and we take captive every*
> *thought to make it obedient to Christ.*
> 2 CORINTHIANS 10:5 (NIV)

This is only possible through God's might. The pathways for such self-deprecating talk are likely deeply entrenched and, as such, will require a tremendous amount of steadfastness. To paraphrase Albert Einstein, we can't solve a problem with the same mind that created it.

> *Don't copy the behavior and customs of this*
> *world, but let God transform you into a new*
> *person by changing the way you think.*
> ROMANS 12:2 (NLT)

Our thought life has tremendous influence on the rest of the areas of our lives but our diet, sleep, and physical activity impact it greatly. To be able to generate healthy thoughts, certain physiological needs must first be met. Diet can play a requisite role in this process. If we consume food-like products that our bodies do not recognize and cannot assimilate, our physiology is compromised. Additionally, if we are regularly consuming inflammatory foods such as sugar, processed foods, soda, and white flour products, our bodies' systems must shift their focus to countering the inflammation brought on by these choices, detracting from more ideal, higher-level functions. This means we cannot even take these life-enhancing measures with the necessary consistency and zeal simply because we are not optimally fueling our bodies. So, recalling my model of wellness, this is why God must be considered in all areas. Before reaching for those problematic foods, take a couple of seconds to first pray for God's strength to decline the food and second to examine how that food choice would affect your stewardship of your physical body, which we know is a treasured gift; so much so that God has chosen, by His Spirit, to reside in each of us. Think of it this way: if you were fortunate enough to have a highly influential person like the president visit your home, would you not frenetically clean, organize, and even decorate so as to present your home in its very best condition? How much more should we consider taking extra special care of our bodies knowing God lives in them?

Or don't you know that your body is the temple of the Holy Spirit, who lives in you and was given to you by God? You do not belong to yourself, for God bought you with a high price. So you must honor God with your body.
1 CORINTHIANS 6:19 (NLT)

We are wired for love, so God's food is designed to meet that need. Local food choices are ideal, considering God placed you there and will provide optimal foods for you to thrive. His expressed love is so multifaceted. Consider *how* you eat in addition to *what* you eat. If you are stressed, rushed, not mindful, slouching, not chewing, angry, sad, and so forth, you will not digest properly. All aspects of God's design must be synchronistic in order to optimally process and metabolize our food. The Standard American Diet (SAD) is quickly causing the majority of Americans, including our children, to suffer a myriad of diseases, resulting in skyrocketing health care issues and costs. Ask yourself if you are among the population of people who are willing to be chained to the idea, propagated by the processed food industry and other self-interest groups, that what we eat does not affect our health and well-being. I implore you to challenge that chain. Only until we take individual responsibility by performing our own due diligence into the impact our food choices are having on our bodies will these giants ever be taken down. If the individuals, one by one, conclude through education that whole, local, seasonal foods are optimal and yield our best health, then the junk food will remain on the shelves which will, in time, eliminate the industry altogether, all through the power of one. That's the ideal.

We can consider sleep in a similar way. If we push ourselves to the brink of exhaustion and deny our bodies the rest they are designed to receive each night, we cannot expect to produce our highest-quality thoughts and remain healthy. Even in His creation account, He added the seventh day for rest. While we know God never tires,

He included a day of rest so that we would model after it. In the Old Testament, we read of God's instruction to allow even the ground to rest every seven years, meaning there would be no planting or harvesting that year so the soil could be replenished and yield high-quality crops in the coming cycles. *"But in the seventh year the land is to have a year of sabbath rest, a sabbath to the LORD. Do not sow your fields or prune your vineyards"* (Leviticus 25:4 [NIV]). Rest is a paramount element to our best life and must therefore be treated as a priority, not a luxury.

Countless medical research studies confirm extended periods of sleep deprivation will likely lead to a host of medical issues and diseases such as irritability, immune system compromise, obesity, high blood pressure, heart disease, and shortened life expectancy.[33] A 2013 Gallup poll showed the average American gets only 6.8 hours of sleep per night, when the nightly recommended number is 8.[34] Those lost 1.2 hours per night add up and, over time, lead to disease. Again, ask yourself if you are chained by false beliefs in this area. Do you view sleep as an unnecessary waste of time? Do you ignore issues that prevent you from quality sleep, like apnea, snoring, excessive caffeine consumption, nighttime use of technology, or restlessness because you've surrendered to the notions "It's just the way it is" or "All that sleep isn't necessary"? Challenge the chain.

The final area of highest priority is physical activity. I personally have evolved into the person I am proud to be today due in large part to regular exercise. I have been running and weight training for over thirty years and will go for as long as my body allows. Running, to me, is a divine experience. As I set out, I center my thoughts and quickly find myself in conversation with God. It is in these moments when I receive the most revelation. It is also my most efficient means to shedding emotional baggage. This experience is very common among runners, inspiring such adages as, "Run till you leave your demons heaving on the side of the road" and "If you want to change your body, exercise. If you want to change your life, become a runner."[35] Dave Griffin shares one of my major motivations for lacing up my sneakers. "When I'm running, I settle my own disputes and comfort my ailing emotions. I don't know why, but answers seem more obvious and problems less troublesome when I'm in motion."

Regardless of your sport of choice, intense physical exercise clears the clutter of your mind, organizes your thoughts, scrapes away exaggerated emotions, and paves the way for logical, productive thinking. I equate it to going for a walk in the woods, which represents a day in the life of all of us. When you emerge, you are covered in stubborn burs, which represent burdens and damaging beliefs that attach themselves to your spirit. I suppose you could choose to ignore those burs and just get on with your life, but each day you "walk through the woods," new burs will attach themselves to you and accumulate. Eventually, you will become so overwhelmed by the task of cleaning your clothing that you may abandon the responsibility altogether and instead walk around a filthy mess. Ideally, those with a determination to rid themselves of stubborn hitchhikers moment by moment will not proceed until they've plucked off every bur.

Exercise is the ultimate bur remover and is a sure-fire way to stave off depression and anxiety. There is a wealth of scientific research confirming the medicinal health benefits of regular physical exercise. According to the Anxiety and Depression Association of America, "Regular exercise works as well as medication for some people to reduce symptoms of anxiety and depression, and the effects can be long lasting."[36] Science confirming God's design and biblical truths once again (1 Corinthians 9:26–27).

> Lack of activity destroys the good
> condition of every human being, while
> movement and methodical physical
> exercise save it and preserve it.
> —PLATO

Like all the areas of life depicted in the Wellness Pyramid, there is a true bio-individual component. While I prefer intense, pounding movement to shake loose the burs that cling, others might prefer slow, more gentle movement to accomplish the same goal. Regardless of intensity preference, consider prioritizing physical activity into your everyday to keep your spirit free of burs and your communication pathway to God clear. Most of us know there are multiple health risks associated with inactivity which include obesity, heart disease, bone loss, muscle atrophy, depression, anxiety, and compromised mobility. But for many, that data is not enough to inspire the new habit of daily exercise. The most common excuse I hear is, "I just don't have the time." I submit that everyone's day can be evaluated to recover precious time lost to dawdling and random bits of doing.

> Let us 'redeem the time.' Random
> working, fitful planning, irregular reading,
> ill-assorted hours, careless or delayed
> execution of business, hurry and bustle,
> loitering and unpreparedness—these,
> and the like, are the things which take
> out the whole purpose and power from
> life, which hinder holiness, and which
> eat like a canker into our moral being.
> —HORATIUS BONAR

Our actions, not our words, reveal what our priorities truly are. If being healthy were, in fact, a priority, we would see to it that exercise fit into our daily routine. We all seem to make plenty of time for checking social media and watching some television. In fact, it's estimated that Americans age eighteen through sixty-four spend an average of 3.2 hours per day online trolling social networking sites![37] If you would steal back just forty-five minutes and exercise instead, you would decrease your chances for lifestyle-related diseases and even premature death exponentially![38] The health benefits are plentiful and include reduced risk of certain cancers, increased skeletal strength, increased muscularity, overall strength, stamina, lower blood pressure, a positive mood and outlook, better quality sleep, and longer life expectancy.[39]

I can testify to the claim that setting and achieving physical goals causes you to feel powerful in every way and affords the courage necessary to reach even higher. It was only after completing my first marathon that I seriously considered the possibility of starting my own health coaching business and authoring a book. You are reading this now because I stepped out in faith and said yes to a then terrifying goal of running 26.2 miles. As with all areas of life, evaluate your beliefs relating to exercise. Are they limiting you and setting you up for health issues? Are you missing out on robust energy and physical health in exchange for more time on the couch? I pray the scales drop from your eyes and the enemy's influence over your thinking and choices is revealed. Challenge the chain.

In my opinion, while all sixteen areas of my Wellness Pyramid are indeed needs, they funnel upward in terms of their criticalness or urgency with regards to our health. Having attained the pinnacle of wellness is to meet, balance, and maintain all sixteen needs in full reliance on God, reaching the top of your wellness pyramid. In partnership with God and a faith-based health coach, I know this is possible because for every Goliath, there is a stone.

Conclusion

Now that you have pondered the preferred ways of both the elephant and a biblical hero like David, it is time to choose which you will be. Are you tired of the drudgery and hopelessness that accompany paltry thinking? God created animals with a ceiling, so the elephant will ever only progress so far, whereas human beings were created in His image and therefore have limitless potential. With that, His heart is to see us ever growing, expanding, and striving for fullness and understanding. Don't model the ways of the elephant, accepting what was told to you as a young child, or at any point in your life for that matter, that does not align with God's truths. Instead, go to God's Word for guidance on how to recognize strongholds in your life, claim authority over them through the power of the name of Jesus Christ, and step out in faith into the life God planned for you all along! He must be your center, your core. We must be ever drawn to Him, as if magnetized, permitting this world to only entice us so far before returning to that nucleus.

Compare this to tetherball. The pole is grounded and immovable, representing God. The string, representing the Holy Spirit, is affixed on one end to that pole and on the other to the ball, which represents us. The ball can only oscillate so far, held close to the pole by the string. Forces may impact the ball with great might, but the string will not let go. It insists the ball remain attached to the pole. Once you belong to God, absolutely nothing can separate you from Him.

> *And I am convinced that nothing can ever separate us from God's love. Neither death nor life, neither angels nor demons, neither our fears for today nor our worries about tomorrow—not even the powers of hell can separate us from God's love. No power in the sky above or in the earth below—indeed, nothing in all creation will ever be able to separate us from the love of God that is revealed in Christ Jesus our Lord.*
> ROMANS 8:38–39 (NLT)

As you work, don't be swayed by backsliding and error. It's all part of the human experience. Paul, the author of nearly two-thirds of the New Testament, struggled the same as you and I.

> *I don't understand myself at all, for I really want to do what is right, but I don't do it. Instead, I do the very thing I hate. I know perfectly well that what I am doing is wrong,*

*and my bad conscience shows that I agree
that the law is good...No matter which way
I turn, I can't make myself do right. I want
to, but I can't. When I want to do good,
I don't. And when I try not to do wrong,
I do it anyway...Oh, what a miserable
person I am! Who will free me from this
life that is dominated by sin? Thank God!
The answer is in Jesus Christ our Lord.*
ROMANS 7:15–16,18–19, 24–25 (NLT)

I find it very refreshing knowing Paul also struggled with moving from his head to his heart, which is vital to effecting lasting change in our behaviors. But he reveals the answer to this conundrum we all struggle with, and it's Christ. Chinese philosopher Han Feizi observed, "Knowing the facts is easy. Knowing how to act based on the facts is difficult." I'm sure you would agree with his wisdom. It's why partnership is so integral to the process of eliminating ruinous habits and replacing them with healthy ones. When we are held accountable and encouraged in love, our chances of success increase exponentially. We must conclude that the only way to finally put to death all our wrong, self-destructive choices is to invite God's power into our lives. Evil sneaks in quietly through the unlocked backdoor of our spirits and culture. Once inside, it surreptitiously maneuvers about, cunningly eroding our standards for living.

Over just the past half century, much has been under attack: marriage, the family unit, family mealtime, home cooking, Sabbath days of rest, time spent with family and friends, eight-hour work days and five-day work weeks, local farms, spirituality and faith, physical activity (especially among the youth), access to quality whole foods, clean drinking water, and authority of all types—just to list a few. Each of these is fundamental to living our best lives. The fading away of such gifts has been slow enough to go undetected by the masses. Consider listening to Paul Harvey's broadcast "If I Were the Devil," which has prophetic wisdom birthed long before its time.[40] Today many are either scrambling to reclaim some semblance of normalcy and rhythm or, worse yet, simply abandoning the whole lot for the sake of utter frustration leading to societal ruin. But, if you have Jesus, neither of these reactions is an option. You can instead trust in the sovereign master plan of God and stay your appointed course for however long He sees fit to keep you here, all the while striving to love yourself and others as best as you possibly can.

To do that, surveying each of the lifestyle areas of the Wellness Pyramid for weakness, forging, and ultimately living out a solid plan for balance and even mastery is of the utmost importance. Like applying your breathing mask before your neighbor's in the event of an aircraft emergency, address your vulnerabilities first. That is how you not only love yourself well but also those in your life because they are interacting with the very best version of you. So, you see, self-love and care are not selfish. Just the opposite is true—they are selfless when pursued with righteous, God-honoring motivation.

Each day, as we migrate toward healing and wholeness, we take a step closer to the cross through a process called sanctification. As disciples, our ultimate pursuit is for ever-increasing Spirit fruit as strongholds lose their grip and fade away. We will never reach the perfection God originally designed us to have until we leave this life and enter into eternity with Him. Remember, "Satan not only delights in the moment of our sin, but also in the spiritual paralysis that ensnares us afterwards."[41] Don't give the enemy satisfaction twice! Acknowledge and repent of your sin and move forward in victory, lest your life speak vanity over Christ's finished work. God is not like the elephant that remembers offenses for decades and seeks revenge. The very moment you confess, the offense is cast as far as the east is from the west, never to be reconsidered again (Psalm 103:12). *That's* the God we serve! So, when we pick up that which God has already laid down, we tell Him that His sacrifice was insufficient; that He is not enough to render your slate clean.

Everyone you encounter is observing your life and reconciling your actions to your words, most especially your family. If you say you believe, then live like it! While Peter was addressing wives in this verse, I believe his wisdom applies to us all. *"Your godly lives will speak to them better than any words. They will be won over by watching your pure, godly behavior"* (1 Peter 3:1-2 [NLT]). Get excited about the renewing work God is preparing to do in you, noting He allows giants in our lives to draw out the David in each of us. Rise and get on with the work God has assigned you, namely loving God, yourself, and others. While, for now, you may be chained by certain strongholds, know that *"the word of God cannot be chained"* (2 Timothy 2:9 [NLT]). It is the only force strong enough to break every chain! If you begin this journey of change in true, committed partnership, you will not fail. You cannot fail because *"If God is for us, who can be against us?"* (Romans 8:31[NIV]). So partner with God, collect your stones, set your sights on your giants, and watch Him bring you from "chained" to "changed"!

> *What counts is whether we really have been*
> *changed into new and different people.*
> GALATIANS 6:15 (NLT)

Be not discouraged because of your soul's
enemies. Are you troubled with thoughts,
fears, doubts, imaginations, reasonings?
Do you see, yet, much in you, excited
to the power of life? Oh! Do not fear it;
do not look at it, so as to be discouraged
by it, but look to Him! Look up to the
power which is over all their strength;
wait for the descending of the power
upon you; adobe in faith of the Lord's
help, and wait in patience till the Lord
arise; ***and see if His arms do not scatter***
what yours could not. So, be still before
Him, and, in stillness, believe in His
name; yes, enter not into the hurrying
of the enemy, though they fill the soul;
for, there is yet some places to which
they cannot enter, from where patience,
faith, and hope will spring up in you,
even in the midst of all they can do.
—ISAAC PENINGTON

ABOUT THE AUTHOR

Slingshot Health Coaching Maxim
"Heal the Family, Heal the World"

She did not try to set others right;
she only listened to and loved and
understood her fellow-creatures.
—ELIZA KEARY

My name is Tracy Ann Spiaggia and I am a Certified Health Coach through the Institute for Integrative Nutrition (IIN), a Certified Personal Trainer and Child Fitness Specialist through American Fitness Professionals and Associates (AFPA), a Certified Running Coach through Road Runners Club of America (RRCA), and a Blessing Champion through Light University with my BA in Family and Child Studies. I specialize in the intersection of spirituality and wellness while prioritizing the thought life, using my gift of encouragement to lead others into healthier lifestyles with God at the center. My heart is to see families flourish, which, in my view, is the most formidable means to counter the erosion of society. The family is made strong by a returning to God as our authority, living according to His precepts, and loving as Christ loved. I believe this is the elixir to our modern-day ills. "Heal the family, heal the world." The message gleaned from the David and Goliath account was the inspiration for creating Slingshot Health Coaching. I can relate to David's characteristics of intensity and passion and believe that God will use them for His glory in my life just as He did in David's. It is my earnest prayer that I can be used by God to motivate my clients into their own valleys and to empower them to do battle without fear or hesitation, trusting that the Almighty has gone before them and will deliver victory. I am expecting great things from God as I love others with my life by communicating my heartfelt message of restoration through faith, education, and consistent implementation facilitated through partnership and effective coaching.

> The creative religious thinker is not
> a daydreamer, not an ivory tower
> intellectual carrying on his lofty
> cogitations remote from the rough
> world; he is more likely to be a troubled,
> burdened man weighed down by
> the woes of existence, occupied not
> with matters academic or theoretical
> but the practical and personal.
> —A.W. TOZER

RESOURCES

Below are the links to two songs that poignantly speak to the truths provided in this book. I encourage you to still your hearts and minds, read through the inspired lyrics, listen to the songs, and watch the videos, allowing it all to wash over you. These artists, I believe, have been gifted to create music that possesses fantastic emotion, declaration, and transformational power. I pray these songs bring the message of my book even deeper into your spirit.

Giants Fall
Battistelli, Francesca, and Matt Hammitt. *Giants Fall*. Word Entertainment and Fervent Records, 2014. MP3.
http://francescamusic.com
https://www.youtube.com/watch?v=A6LVkcfgmnc

Chain Breaker
Williams, Zach. *Chain Breaker*. Essential Records, 2017. MP3.
http://zachwilliamsmusic.com
https://www.youtube.com/watch?v=cd_xxmXdQz4

I have included the websites of all the brilliant leaders I referenced on the Acknowledgements page. It is wise to "eat" of God's full and diverse table of teachers, for they each offer unique perspectives that we might not attain on our own. By this, each of us turns the prism of God ever so slightly with every new understanding, knowing and enjoying Him more fully as we grow. Nothing compares to discovering God for yourself through quiet, regular study of His word, but we are designed for fellowship and discovering God's full nature through relationship with one another and in the sharing of our testimonies. So, I encourage you to supplement your independent study with wisdom from minds such as these.

Oswald Chambers	https://utmost.org
A.W. Tozer	https://www.cmalliance.org/about/history/tozer
C.S. Lewis	http://www.cslewis.com/us/
Dr. Gary Smalley	http://www.smalley.cc
Dr. Timothy Keller	http://www.timothykeller.com
Dr. Ravi Zacharias	http://rzim.org
Andy Stanley	http://northpoint.org/messages
Jimmy Evans	http://marriagetoday.com
Dr. Caroline Leaf	http://drleaf.com
Gary Thomas	http://www.garythomas.com
Joyce Meyer	https://www.joycemeyer.org
Dr. John Trent	http://strongfamilies.com

CITATIONS

1. *Preventing Chronic Diseases: A Vital Investment.* Geneva: World Health Organization, 2005. ISBN 92 4 156300 1. *World Health Organization.* WHO Press, 2005. Web. 17 Jan. 2017.

2. The Power of Prevention, Chronic disease . . . the public health challenge of the 21st century, National Center for Chronic Disease Prevention and Health Promotion, 2009, p.1

3. "Why Good Nutrition Is Important | Center for Science in the Public Interest." *Why Good Nutrition Is Important | Center for Science in the Public Interest.* N.p., n.d. Web. 20 Jan. 2017. <https://cspinet.org/eating-healthy/why-good-nutrition-important>.

4. Merriam Webster

5. Alban, Deane. "Epigenetics: How You Can Change Your Genes And Change Your Life." *Reset.me.* N.p., 18 Feb. 2016. Web. 17 Jan. 2017.; Dr. Caroline Leaf; Joseph M., Dr. "Epigenetics: How Your Mind Can Reprogram Your Genes." *Mercola.com.* N.p., 11 Apr. 2012. Web. 17 Jan. 2017.

6. http://drleaf.com

7. Exodus 20:1-6, 34:7; Numbers 14:8; Deuteronomy 5:9; Switch On Your Brain, Dr. Caroline Leaf, pp.56-61

8. Heldoorn, Kendall. "5 Traits That Prove Elephants Are Gentle Giants." *The Dodo*. N.p., 17 Apr. 2015. Web. 17 Jan. 2017.

9. Highfield, Roger. "Www.smh.com.au." Elephant Rage: They Never Forgive, Either - World. N.p., 17 Feb. 2006. Web. 17 Jan. 2017.

10. "Www.elephantsforever.co.za." *Elephant Rage*. N.p., n.d. Web. 17 Jan. 2017. <http://www.elephantsforever.co.za/elephant-rage.html>.

11. Highfield, Roger. "Www.smh.com.au." Elephant Rage: They Never Forgive, Either - World. N.p., 17 Feb. 2006. Web. 17 Jan. 2017.

12. LaBracio, Lisa. "12 Amazing Facts about Elephants." *TED-Ed Blog*. N.p., 11 Aug. 2015. Web. 17 Jan. 2017.

13. "Do elephants never forget?" 5 August 2008. HowStuffWorks.com. <http://animals.howstuffworks.com/mammals/elephant-memory.htm> 17 January 2017; "UK | Scotland | Edinburgh, East and Fife | Elephants Sense 'danger' Clothes." *BBC News*. BBC, 18 Oct. 2007. Web. 17 Jan. 2017.

14. Frei, Georges. "Elephant Training in the Zoo and Circus." *Upalich*. N.p., 20 Nov. 2016. Web. 17 Jan. 2017.

15. "Mahout." *Wikipedia*. Wikimedia Foundation, n.d. Web. 17 Jan. 2017.

16. Frei, Georges. "Elephant Training in the Zoo and Circus." *Upalich*. N.p., 20 Nov. 2016. Web. 17 Jan. 2017.

17. "Elephant Crushing." *Wikipedia*. Wikimedia Foundation, n.d. Web. 17 Jan. 2017.

18. "Facts About Elephants." *Facts About Elephants*. N.p., n.d. Web. 17 Jan. 2017. <http://www.elephantstay.com/Facts-about-elephants.html>.

19. Romans 10:9

20. Lewis, C. S. *The Screwtape Letters*. London: G. Bles, Centenary, 1942. 67. Print.

21. Ezekiel 28:12-14

22. Lewis, C. S. *The Screwtape Letters*. London: G. Bles, Centenary, 1942. 61. Print.

23. Press, Summerside. *Alone in God's Presence: A 365 Daily Devotional Journal*. Place of Publication Not Identified: Summerside Pr, 2011. Print.

24. "SourceFlix | Living Hope." *SourceFlix Living Hope*. N.p., n.d. Web. 18 Jan. 2017.

25. Matthew 4:1-11

26. James 4:7

27. "100 Bible Verses about Power Of Words." *What Does the Bible Say About Power Of Words?* N.p., n.d. Web. 17 Jan. 2017. <https://www.openbible.info/topics/power_of_words>.

28. Staff, Mayo Clinic. "Forgiveness: Letting Go of Grudges and Bitterness." *Mayo Clinic.* N.p., 11 Nov. 2014. Web. 17 Jan. 2017.

29. Leaf, Caroline. Switch On Your Brain: The Key to Peak Happiness, Thinking, and Health. Grand Rapids, MI: Baker, 2013. Print.

30. Luke 15

31. Psalm 103:12 (NLT)

32. Press, Summerside. *Alone in God's Presence: A 365 Daily Devotional Journal.* Place of Publication Not Identified: Summerside Pr, 2011. Print.

33. Pietrangelo, Ann, and George Krucik, MD MBA. "Effects of Sleep Deprivation on the Body." *Healthline.* N.p., 19 Aug. 2014. Web. 17 Jan. 2017.

34. Gallup, Inc. "In U.S., 40% Get Less Than Recommended Amount of Sleep." *Gallup.com.* N.p., 19 Dec. 2013. Web. 17 Jan. 2017.

35. Author Unknown

36. Otto, Michael W., PhD, and Jasper A.J. Smits, PhD. "Exercise for Stress and Anxiety." *Anxiety and Depression Association of America, ADAA*. N.p., July 2014. Web. 17 Jan. 2017.

37. Staff, MarketingCharts. "Social Networking Eats Up 3+ Hours Per Day For The Average American User." *MarketingCharts*. N.p., 09 Jan. 2013. Web. 17 Jan. 2017.

38. "Physical Activity and Health." *Centers for Disease Control and Prevention*. Centers for Disease Control and Prevention, 04 June 2015. Web. 17 Jan. 2017.; "American Heart Association Recommendations for Physical Activity in Adults." *American Heart Association Recommendations for Physical Activity in Adults*. N.p., 27 July 2016. Web. 17 Jan. 2017.

39. "Risks of Physical Inactivity." *Risks of Physical Inactivity | Johns Hopkins Medicine Health Library*. N.p., n.d. Web. 17 Jan. 2017. <http://www.hopkinsmedicine.org/healthlibrary/conditions/cardiovascular_diseases/risks_of_physical_inactivity_85, p00218/>.

40. Bctvguy. "If I Were the Devil - (BEST VERSION) by PAUL HARVEY Audio Restored." *YouTube*. YouTube, 23 Mar. 2012. Web. 17 Jan. 2017. <https://www.youtube.com/watch?v=H3Az0okaHig>.

41. Author unknown

40254660R00077

Made in the USA
Middletown, DE
26 March 2019